DATE D

STARS UPSTREAM

STARS

UPSTREAM

LIFE ALONG AN OZARK RIVER

BY LEONARD HALL

UNIVERSITY OF MISSOURI PRESS ● COLUMBIA

Standard Book Number 8262–0074–5
Library of Congress Card Number 59–5772
Copyright © 1958 by
The University of Chicago Press
First publication 1958
Second impression 1961
All rights reserved
Permission to publish paperback edition
granted 1969 by the copyright holders
to the
University of Missouri Press
Revised edition © 1969 by
The Curators of the University of Missouri
Manufactured in the United States of America

FOREWORD

The paperback edition of *Stars Upstream* is long over-due. This story of the Current River in the Missouri Ozarks belongs on every drugstore book rack as well as in every library. It will bring Americans closer to their outdoor heritage.

When this book first appeared in 1958, Ira N. Gabrielson, biologist, conservationist, and author, said in his Foreword: "*Stars Upstream* should be required reading for everyone interested in the future of America."

Nothing has happened in the past decade to change that judgment. On the contrary, steady increases in the leisure time of our people, in population pressures, park use, environmental pollution, and urbanization of the countryside make *Stars Upstream* more appropriate reading today than ever.

The author tells of man's exploitation and misuse of outdoor America, but he retains an innate optimism that much of the natural beauty that man has so nearly destroyed can be saved. And in his native Ozark country, there has occurred an event of major proportions to fulfill that hope, the successful effort to preserve the Current River not only for the people of Missouri but for the entire country.

Congress authorized in 1964 an Ozark National Scenic Riverways designed to include some 85,000 acres of the Current and Jacks Fork rivers as an elongated, wild river park. Both rivers are almost legendary for their clean, blue-green waters and unde-

spoiled scenery. And it was *Stars Upstream* that awakened its readers to the danger of losing their wild rivers to commercialism, exploitation, and pollution. In doing so, this book helped to bring Missouri the first national scenic riverways in the National Park System.

It has been my privilege to float "Running River"— *La Rivière Courante* as the early French traders called it—with the author, and we shall, I hope, float it again. This book will serve well any visitor to the new scenic riverways as a wealth of information on the region by a man who knows virtually every rock and rill of the Current and Jacks Fork.

There is a creative parallel between *Stars Upstream* and Ozark National Scenic Riverways. The book preserves in warm descriptive terms the essential beauty, adventure, and meaning of the Current River. Ozark National Scenic Riverways preserves within the National Park System the rivers themselves for all future generations.

Americans and other visitors will travel and re-travel these rivers. And they will read and re-read this exceptional book.

GEORGE B. HARTZOG, JR.
Director, National Park Service

Washington, D.C.
May, 1968

ACKNOWLEDGMENTS

A book such as *Stars Upstream* results from the contributions of many people. There are writers past and present, naturalists, foresters, wildlife technicians, photographers, scientists in a dozen fields. To give full and proper credit to all of them would be impossible; yet the chief contributors should certainly be mentioned.

At the top of the list are those who have, through personal contact or their writings, taught me most about the landscape. Here I would start with the late Aldo Leopold of Wisconsin, whose *A Sand County Almanac* is the most vital statement to date on conservation in America. Close beside him stands the British ecologist Fraser Darling, whose *Pelican in the Wilderness* gives to the layman a sweeping view of the North American continent. The late Rudolf Bennitt who headed the Wildlife Unit at the University of Missouri is another; the *Survey of Resident Game and Furbearers of Missouri*, which he wrote with Werner Nagel of the Missouri Conservation Commission, is drawn upon frequently.

There are others. William Albrecht of the University of Missouri, a great soil scientist and authority on nutrition, has been a constant inspiration during the years we have known him. Then there are Julian Steyermark and Bill Bauer, who have botanized the Ozarks as professional and amateur respectively; Ed Clark and Tom Beveridge, who have served successively as Missouri State Geologist; a dozen forest-

ers at the field level—Buck Hornkohl, Ed Woods, Giff Adams, and others—who have taught me much about the Ozark timber.

It seems that a complete bibliography of the many volumes referred to in preparing such an informal narrative as *Stars Upstream* is hardly necessary. Among those most helpful, however, were Houck's *History of Missouri;* several works by the nineteenth-century historian Schoolcraft; Carl Sauer's *Geography of the Ozark Highland;* Josiah Bridge's *Geology of the Eminence and Cardareva Quadrangles;* Julian Steyermark's *Spring Flora of Missouri.*

During the time the manuscript of *Stars Upstream* was in preparation, I was working on a parallel project—a color film called *An Ozark Anthology,* to be shown for the National Audubon Society. Thus I was forced to forego making all the black-and-white photographs for the book. This was probably a fortunate circumstance, since it forced me to call upon some of Missouri's best photographers for their material on the Current River country, and I am pleased to acknowledge my indebtedness to them.

Charles W. Schwartz of the Missouri Conservation Commission generously allowed the use of photographs 6, 15, 17, 20, 21, 22, 24, 26, 27, 28, and 31. The Missouri Conservation Commission permitted the use of photograph 16, and a member of its staff, Don Wooldridge, receives credit for photographs 18, 23, 25, 29, and 30. Gerald R. Massie of the Missouri Division of Commerce and Industrial Development provided photographs 2, 10, and 32; a colleague, Ralph W. Walker, photographs 4 and 14; Rex Gary, photograph 3; and Hadley K. Irwin of the Missouri State Park Board photographs 1, 11, 13, and 19.

One other person must be mentioned here, although you will come to know her if you read the book. This is Virginia Hall, my wife, who has shared the research, work, and fun that have gone into *Stars Upstream* and has cheerfully performed the task of reading and re-reading the manuscript both silently and aloud. Without her aid and encouragement, her skill with a paddle in the bow of the canoe, her artistry with a frying pan over the campfire—it seems probable that the book would not have gotten itself written.

LEONARD HALL

CONTENTS

RUNNING RIVER

Have you ever sat on a riverbank at night and watched how the reflections of the stars seem to travel upstream against the current?

We were camped one evening down at the mouth of Buffalo Creek on Current River—a place where stars move upstream. There was my wife Ginnie, companion on all my wilderness forays, Dick Moore, who sometimes guides for us when I don't want to do all the paddling and camp chores, and myself. The time was mid-October, when the color on the Ozark hills is at its most brilliant. That afternoon, we had seen the yellow hickories glowing like candle flames on the steep sides of every hollow, and close beside them the sour gums blazed bright red. Dogwoods in the forest understory showed scarlet against the somber dress of the oaks. Little blue asters were in bloom, and the flowers of the cardinal lobelia lined the riverbank.

This Current River, which flows through the eastern Ozarks, is the loveliest of all our Missouri streams and can hold up its head for beauty alongside any on our North American continent. I like best its old French name, *La Riviere Courante*—which is to say, "Running River"—for nothing could better describe the swift course it takes down its wild and narrow valley. It is to be regretted that the first frontiersmen from the mountains of the Appalachian highland who settled here in the early 1800's did not translate the old French

name literally instead of phonetically; yet "Current" is equally descriptive, if not quite as poetic.

Our campsite on this evening lay about halfway along the 150-mile course of the stream and is one of our favorites, perhaps because it can be reached only by canoe or native John-boat. As we pitched the forest-green tent and gathered wood for our cooking fire, an osprey lifted from his sentinel post on a dead snag across the river and soared in ascending circles above us, complaining harshly at this intrusion upon his privacy. A band of blue-winged teal, put to flight by some boatman far upstream, flashed past in the late sunlight with wings whistling in the urgency of their flight.

Let me see if I can picture our campsite for you. Here at the mouth of Buffalo Creek the river flows in a straight course from north to south instead of curving in a typical oxbow. It comes rushing down a clear rapid to plunge into a green pool beneath a towering limestone bluff. The creek itself flows in from the northwest, meeting the river at the upper end of the deep pool. Its mouth forms a bay, a stone's throw wide and perhaps a half-mile long. In this quiet water we often find wild ducks stopping to rest after the autumn migration has begun. And more than once at dusk, just as the bullfrogs start tuning up, we have watched a whitetail buck come down from the dry timbered ridges to drink and browse among the lily pads.

Between the main channel of the river and the bay runs a narrow point of land like a small peninsula that ends in a high gravel bar where the two currents meet at the head of the pool. The lower or downstream end of this bar makes an ideal place to pitch an overnight camp. If rain should come up suddenly, the gravel will

absorb any amount of water without letting a drop run under the tent floor. The site is high enough, moreover, so there is little danger of being caught by a sudden rise of the stream—a contingency that must always be considered in selecting a campsite on an Ozark river. Best of all, the swift-flowing water sings gently past the camp all night long; and this moving current keeps enough air stirring so there is never a mosquito to bother you.

Over to the west of camp the sun sets early behind the trees atop the high bluff, so that even on the hottest summer afternoon the gravel bar is delightfully cool. There is fine swimming in the pool below camp, and after the supper dishes are finished, you can take a camp chair to the tip of the bar if you like and cast a fat chub minnow far out into the current. There is always the chance of hooking a big bass feeding in the dusk or one of the giant walleyes that lurk among the boulders where the water is deepest.

On the October evening of which I write, there was a bit of chill in the air after the stars came out and the mist began to steal up the river. So we pulled on wool shirts and dragged in logs from a big drift above camp and built up a cheerful blaze. Then, because it was too early to sleep and because we hated to leave the warmth of the campfire, we sat back against the bedrolls and listened to tales of early times in Current River valley. Dick Moore has lived here all his days, and most of them have been spent guiding on the river, so that he is an incomparable boatman and a fine outdoor companion as well. Moreover—and in this he is unlike many of his compatriots on the river—Dick can cook a skillet of bass to golden perfection and has a wonderful

faculty for seeing that you roll out of your blankets in the morning to the aroma of fresh-brewed coffee. It is strong coffee, too; for only if the camp axe will dissolve in the brown brew will Dick admit he may have gotten it "a bit too stout."

There were tales told beside the campfire. Tales like the one of how the big panther of Shawnee Creek finally met his fate one day when he was swimming Current River with a half-grown pig in his mouth and had the bad luck to encounter Dick Moore coming downstream in a boat. We heard of the days when the biggest sawmills in America operated here in Current River valley, at nearby Grandin and at West Alley up on Jacks Fork. Countless miles of narrow-gauge railway traversed the forest ridges and followed along the river-bank to haul the logs of virgin pine and oak to the mills to be processed into lumber.

There were stories, too, of the great rafts of railroad ties that used to float down Current River each season. These rafts were made up of individual "squares" of perhaps thirty hand-hewn oak ties, each of which was approximately 6 inches by 8 inches by 8 feet long. The ties were laid crosswise and joined together with oak binding poles spiked with 40-penny nails. When one "square" was completed, a second was built and tied to the first with a coupling pole. Enough space was left between squares so that the raft was flexible and could take the turns in the river. As many as 1,500 ties went into a single raft, which might be 2,000 feet in length.

These rafts were navigated by two or three men who would be on the river for several weeks, since the speed was governed by the current and various obstructions in the river and might not exceed a half-dozen miles per

day. So heavy were the ties that generally the raft pushed out its own channel by sheer weight as it inched along downstream. If an obstruction was met that wouldn't move, however, it was blasted from the stream bed with dynamite.

One rafter rode the front of the craft and the other the stern; and when the tie raft started down over a shoal, the man at the stern snubbed hard with his pole. Then when the bow reached the eddy below, both men poled until they reached the next rapid. Sometimes this could be done simply by setting the pole on the river bottom, leaning hard, and then walking steadily as though on a treadmill until the stern of the raft was reached.

Camp gear, food, and bedrolls were lashed to the bow square and guarded carefully against a possible breakup, since their loss would have worked a real hardship on the crew. Now and then some fisherman from town would come aboard the raft, casting his lure in toward the bank and taking all the time he wanted to work a pool or rapid. In those days, strings of twenty to thirty good bass in a morning were not unusual.

Dick Moore told us tales, that evening, of famous coon hounds and fabulous big bucks and of unforgettable fox hunts and the old-time way of pursuing the wild turkey. This was to slip along jangling a cowbell on one side of a timbered ridge where the birds were known to feed. The sound of the bell did not alarm the big birds, for they had grown used to cattle grazing in the forest. Now and then you would poke your head cautiously over the crest of the ridge to try to spot your quarry.

By this time our fire was dying down, and a thin

moon in the last quarter climbed above the sycamores across the river. It was time to seek the warmth of our bedrolls.

"It's a pity this old river can't talk," said Dick, with a prodigious yawn. "The tales I'm telling aren't anything to what you would hear then."

The thing that Dick forgot, although I think he knows it well enough, is that a river does have a voice. And it has a story to tell—for anyone who will learn its language and then listen with an understanding ear.

RUGGED COUNTRY

An interesting characteristic of the Ozark Mountains is that they run in a generally east to west direction, instead of north to south as is the case with all our other mountain ranges. There are perhaps twenty streams orginating in the Ozark highland that warrant the name "river." Ten of these flow down the northern escarpment in a northeasterly direction to empty into the Missouri or Mississippi. The rest take their course down the southern slope of the mountains and, with the exception of the St. Francis River, which empties directly into the Mississippi, are tributary to White River.

All these little rivers of the Ozarks compare favorably for picturesque beauty to any streams in America. Some of them have been dammed by the Army Engineers or by utility companies to form dead-water impoundments which are biotically less interesting than the undammed streams, even though they offer opportunities for mass recreation and—at least in the early years of impoundment—excellent fishing. The undammed rivers, most of them traversing the wilder regions of the hill country, are still largely unspoiled. They can be seen best by floating downstream on them in a canoe or John-boat. This is, in fact, almost the only way really to enjoy them. Our favorites by far are the Current and its tributary Jacks Fork.

In the nature of things, when we envision the beginnings of a river, we are likely to picture in our minds some tiny rill stealing silently from beneath the slowly

melting foot of a glacier high on some rocky mountain-side. We imagine rill and rivulet working their way steadily downhill, joined now and then by others of their kind until the flow becomes a stream and finally, after many accretions, grows large enough to be called a river.

The source of Current River is quite different. This Ozark stream is born high in the heart of the Missouri hills, and we will be closest to truth if we liken its birth to that of Minerva, who sprang full-grown and armored from the head of Jove. In a small and densely wooded valley in the southeast corner of Dent County, steep Crabtree Hollow and Pigeon Creek join together to create a level, parklike area. On the floor of this park, which is no more than a few acres in extent, rise nearly a dozen springs of crystal clarity. Some emerge from the gravel beds which form the valley floor; others flow from among the rocks piled at the base of the surrounding hills.

Since the outlets of all these springs are hardly more than a few yards apart, they are given a single name—Montauk Springs. Together they flow approximately 45 million gallons per day, enough water to form a river of quite respectable size. It would be enough water, in fact, to furnish an ample supply for a small city. But since even the nearest village on its banks lies almost a hundred miles downstream, Current River goes dancing along its steep course clean and undefiled.

Like most other major rivers of the Ozark highland, the Current follows a sharply winding channel which elsewhere would be unusual for a stream of its size, depth, and average fall. Yet it is these very twists and turns and oxbow bends—called "entrenched meanders"

by the geologists—which enable us to place the Ozark rivers in time and know something of their beginnings. In the Cretaceous period—between 60 and 120 million years ago, when the dinosaurs were passing into extinction and the very earliest ancestors of such modern mammals as our horse were beginning to appear—much of the Ozark area had been worn down by erosion into a comparatively level plain from the mountain uplift of an earlier age. Over this plain moved sluggish streams that cut crooked and meandering channels, much like the one which the Mississippi River follows today. When the next great earth disturbance came to push the region upward again, the Ozark streams held largely to their old courses. Gradually they cut their way downward through the softer sedimentary rocks to carve deep valleys; and these valleys twist and wind as did the ancient river channels on the level plain.

Millions of Gallons a Day

Many things about the Current make it unique and help to account for its unusual charm and beauty. With its single surface tributary Jacks Fork, the river drains a rugged and precipitous watershed embracing some 2,500 square miles. Except for Jacks Fork and a few small creeks with uncertain flow, Current River receives more than 60 per cent of its water from the springs which rise along its valley. There are hundreds of these, with flows ranging from a few gallons a day to the tremendous 480 million gallons poured in each 24 hours by Big Spring at Van Buren, reputed to be the largest single-outlet spring in America. Many of the

springs have flows in excess of 25 million gallons, and only the Snake River in Idaho can equal the Current in the number and volume of flow of large springs rising along its valley.

As might be expected of such a spring-fed stream, Current River remains remarkably clear throughout the year except for the occasional rise which follows a hard rain. Its flow is also quite uniform in all seasons, with a much smaller drop during dry periods than other Ozark streams, because the large springs vary little in their volume of discharge. Only long cycles of drought or more than normal rainfall affect them to any extent. The water temperature of Current River remains fairly constant, pleasantly cool in summer and warmer than one would expect in winter. This is because the temperature of the large springs changes no more than a degree or two from their 58-degree average throughout the entire year.

Not many Ozark springs have English names as colorful as those given them by the Osage Indians who were the early inhabitants of this region and to whom beautiful Blue Spring was the Spring of the Summer Sky. Pioneering Anglo-Saxons were more likely to come up with something practical and prosaic such as "Big" or "Cold" or "Round." Yet now and then, as when they named Pulltight Spring, they did manage one that had a tang to it.

Perhaps one reason most of the springs have ordinary, workaday names is that there are so many of them. You could hardly expect a hard-working frontiersman, hewing out a hill farm with his axe or busy at trapping mink and beaver, to take time searching the classics for poetical names. If the spring at the head of his hollow fur-

nished an unfailing supply of water for his woman's wash kettles and his livestock—and perhaps to operate a small still—this was all he asked. Thus we find four "Big," four "Roaring," eight "Blue," and three "Falling" among the large springs of the Ozarks. But we find only one each for the more picturesque "Paydown," "Pulltight," "King Bee," and "Slabtown."

Three other states—Florida, Idaho, and Oregon—can boast springs that are comparable in size to those rising in the Ozark highland of Missouri. It is doubtful, however, that any other state can match Missouri in the total number of its large springs, many of which are small rivers in themselves, or in the beauty of their settings.

What constitutes a "large" spring depends pretty much on the part of the country you are talking about. There are areas where one with a flow of a million gallons per day would be considered extraordinary, attracting visitors from miles around. In the Ozark highland of Missouri there are no less than 150 springs with flows regularly measured at from 1 million to 840 million gallons per day, and countless others would be classed as large if they occurred almost anywhere else in the United States. Dozens of these springs—and among them some of the loveliest—are so isolated that they are seen only by the occasional hunter or back-country cattleman as he rides the timber to salt his livestock.

Although no two of the Current River springs are exactly alike, one thing they have in common is beauty of setting. Some of them flow from the foot of a towering limestone bluff at the water's edge or from gravel beds in the stream itself. Some issue from caves. Some

are born far back in the forest, and others rise in the midst of meadows on little mountain farms. Many of them—like Big Spring—come boiling from the rocks in a torrent. Some—like Blue Spring—rise so silently from their deep and transparent pools that a flow of millions of gallons is indicated only by the gentle stirring of the long fronds of water plants far down in the depths. All the springs are clear and cold and are surrounded by a picturesque and rugged terrain to create scenes of rare and wild beauty.

The combination of mountains, swift-flowing streams, and crystal springs makes the Ozark region an ideal recreational area for the sportsman, vacationist, and nature lover. On Current River alone, the sites of four of the largest springs—Montauk, Round, Alley, and Big Spring—have lent themselves to development as attractive and well-appointed State Parks. Some of the other springs lie within the boundaries of State and National Forests. The rest are privately owned and have been developed as cottage sites, or to supply the water for farm homes, or in a few instances as part of the attraction of resorts and lodges open to the public.

Some of the most beautiful springs are quite inaccessible, and several of the large ones can be visited only by those who float the river. But there are a number that can be reached easily and in comfort over well-improved state highways. A tour of three or four days in the Current River area will enable the traveler to visit a half-dozen of the large springs, and this is a pilgrimage made by many midwesterners each year.

It is impossible not to speculate on the source of the inexhaustible flow of clear, cold water which supplies these large springs. The answer, of course, lies in a com-

bination of climate and geography and geology. All supplies of water, whether on the surface or underground, depend eventually upon rainfall. In the Ozarks the dominant rock structure takes the form of layers of dolomite limestone laid down above the granite and porphyry by successive ocean inundations. The soil structure above the linestone generally contains large quantities of chert or flinty rock which makes this area of the soil horizon quite porous.

During the several upheavals that created the Ozark highland, the limestone layers (some of which are upward of 500 feet thick) have been broken and faulted. Thus when rain falls, it percolates down through the rocky soil layer. From here some of it is taken up by plants and some flows directly out into surface streams. But part of it also finds the cracks or faults in the limestone rocks and continues its course downward into the earth. And here an interesting process goes forward through the ages. Water seeping downward through the soil picks up organic matter and becomes mildly acid. The limestone rock which it penetrates is slightly soluble in acid solutions. Thus very slowly the surface water working downward begins to dissolve the rock. Small hollows are created which finally become caverns, and the water, working its way through fissures in the limestone, joins these one to another until underground streams are born, fed by many collecting reservoirs.

Meanwhile on the surface, the rivers cut their way slowly downward in ancient beds, widening their valleys and changing course where they meet little resistance and cutting narrow canyons or "shut-ins" through the harder stone. Finally the surface river

crosses the course of a subterranean stream—or comes close enough to it so that the underground water finds its way out through some fissure in the rock—and thus a new spring is born.

Many theories are advanced to account for the quantity of this underground water which comes pouring forth. It has been argued that the water may come from the surface rivers themselves or from such distant sources as the Great Lakes or the Rockies. The answer lies in the ages: in normal precipitation over millions upon millions of years, with water ever filtering downward into the reservoirs deep underground. Not too much is known about the reserves of ground water, but we are certain that the quantities thus stored amount in volume to several times the surface water in all our lakes and streams. Nor is this water lost, except for the comparatively small amounts emerging as springs and natural artesian lakes and wells, until man starts to tap and pump it for such purposes as irrigation.

There are tall tales told along Current River valley about the depth of the large springs. A favorite one is of the heavy anvil lowered into the water with all the rope that can be gathered together in the countryside. According to this legend, the anvil descends to a certain depth and finally dances up and down with the pressure of the emerging water, but never has it plumbed the bottom. Hydrologic fact is simpler. Most of the springs have a depth of about 50 feet and an average temperature of 58 degrees Farenheit with a variation of less than a degree from summer to winter. This is close to the 56-degree mean temperature of the region and indicates that the water comes from depths where it is unaffected by seasonal change.

Since the limestone formations of the Ozark highland can be accurately charted for age by the fossils they contain, it is even possible to determine the formations in which the springs originate. Thus Big, Welch, Cave, and Blue Spring emerge from the Eminence limestone which dates back to late Cambrian or very early Ordovician times, some 400 million years ago; while other large springs come from the Van Buren and Gasconade formations that are a mere 250 to 350 million years old. Apparently none of the very large springs originate in more recent limestone deposits.

Although Montauk Springs, which forms the headwaters of Current River, will be mentioned along with others as we float downstream in our canoe, it might be well to touch on the rest of the large springs. This we will do by listing them in their order of occurrence and including those which rise along Jacks Fork.

WELCH SPRING, or WELCH CAVE SPRING, is located some 20 miles downstream from Montauk and 6 or 7 miles below the little village of Cedar Grove near the Current River headwaters. It issues from a cave at the foot of a limestone bluff in a still pool, with an average flow of 100 million gallons per day, and runs down for about a quarter-mile before joining the river. The spring is privately owned and operated as a trout-fishing club by a group of St. Louis sportsmen, but it can be visited by permission.

CAVE SPRING is perhaps 6 miles below Welch Spring and 3 miles downstream from the tiny settlement of Akers. It also issues from a large cave in a bluff at the river's edge and can be entered and traversed for a short distance by boat, since the cave opening is 15 feet or more in height. The location is extremely scenic

but difficult to reach except by river, so that it is seldom visited. Flow measurements vary but probably average 30 million gallons per day.

PULLTIGHT SPRING is located some 8 miles upstream from the point where Highway 19 crosses Current River. It emerges from the base of a bluff in a wooded valley and flows about a half-mile to join the river. The spring is privately owned, and there is a clubhouse nearby. There is no direct access by road; the club members come in to the opposite side of the river on a primitive ridge road and cross by boat with their supplies and equipment. Flow measurements average perhaps 35 million gallons per day. The spring has small supplementary outlets in the gravel of the river bed and at the base of a nearby bluff several hundred yards from the main spring. Pulltight Spring has a remarkably beautiful and rugged setting which will probably not be exploited for a long time.

ROUND SPRING lies near the crossing of Highway 19 and Current River. This large and picturesque spring with a flow of about 40 million gallons per day is the location of a small but attractive State Park. It has obviously been created by the collapse of a cavern roof many years ago, and though the name has little romance about it, Round Spring at least describes very accurately the deep, circular, vertical-walled pool. The source of water here is much more obvious than at many of the springs, for nearby Spring Valley drains a very large watershed yet runs dry throughout the year except for short periods after heavy rain. Such dry valleys where all of the water goes underground are of common occurrence in the Ozarks and are an important source of water for the large springs. Nearby are a

lodge and the well-developed Round Spring Caverns.

ALLEY SPRING is located on Jacks Fork some 6 miles from the town of Eminence and 12 miles up from the mouth of this stream. It is the site of an attractive State Park with comfortable cottages, a lodge, and a well-policed campground. There is excellent swimming and good fishing in the river nearby. The spring rises in a deep, still pool at the foot of a towering bluff of Gasconade limestone in a wooded valley and flows a half-mile before joining the river. The pool is confined by an old dam which once powered a gristmill and saw-mill, and the mill building has been preserved as a museum. Alley Spring has many interesting and unusual features, and the Park is visited each year by thousands of vacationists.

EBB-AND-FLOW SPRING is located far up toward the head of Jacks Fork and is listed here because of its uniqueness rather than its size. This is a periodic spring with a flow somewhat resembling that of a geyser except that there is no gas present or any change in the water temperature. There are 5 such springs in Missouri and only 23 in the United States. This particular spring, also known as Rhymer Spring, builds up to peak flow about once each 24 hours, then subsides again. One theory is that it rises in a syphon formation in the limestone and that the syphon flushes when filled, a process which may take hours, days, or even weeks, depending on the individual spring. The average flow of this particular spring is probably about 2 million gallons per day.

BLUE SPRING is located on Current River about 3 miles downstream from Powder Mill, where the ferry on Highway 106 crosses the stream. For the Indians this

was the Spring of the Summer Sky, and it is now considered by many to be the most beautiful in the entire Ozark highland. It rises in a deep, still pool beneath a high limestone bluff perhaps a half-mile back from the river. When clear, the water has an intense blue color which actually seems to fill the narrow valley with a blue halation. As for translucence, it is often possible during midsummer or autumn to drop a white stone quietly into the water and watch it go drifting slowly down until it comes to rest on the bottom, some 50 feet below. The spring has a flow of about 80 million gallons per day. Although privately owned, it is open to the public. Close beside it, but not on the same property, is Blue Spring Lodge.

GRAVEL SPRING is another spring located in extremely rugged surroundings and accessible only to the boatman floating the river. This unique spring, with a flow of perhaps 40 million gallons, boils up out of a gravel bar at the river's edge and out of the river bed itself. One can lie on the gravel and put his ear to it and hear the sound of a mighty spring bubbling up far beneath him.

BIG SPRING is, as stated, the site of one of Missouri's most popular State Parks. It is located on Current River about 4 miles downstream from Van Buren, seat of government for Carter County and headquarters for many recreationists visiting the Current River country. Largest single-outlet spring in the United States, Big Spring is a magnificent sight as it comes gushing forth from the base of its limestone bluff to pour down its spring branch—actually a small river—and join the parent stream.

The Illusion of Wilderness

One thing which makes Current River unique is that it lives out its entire life within the heart of the Ozark highland and thus is always in character. The watershed which it drains is almost entirely forested, the terrain being so rugged that at least 85 per cent of the land is suited to no other use than the growing of trees. The valley down which it flows is consistently narrow, with only occasional bits of alluvial plain to support small farms that can hardly ever rise above the subsistence level. Despite a record abuse of both forest and agricultural lands which can hardly bring joy to the heart of the conservationist, Current River valley retains the illusion of unspoiled wilderness. Only the trained eye of the ecologist will mark the scars of man's hard hand on this landscape.

When Current River leaves its 150-mile course through the mountains and issues onto the level Arkansas plain, it joins almost at once with two other Ozark rivers—the Black and the Eleven Point. From this juncture the three flow placidly down to White River and so into the parent Mississippi. Up to the point where it leaves Missouri, however, there is little that is placid about the Current. The elevation at Montauk Springs, the source of the river, is 1,000 feet above sea level; while that at the mouth is approximately 250 feet. If this drop of 750 feet in 150 miles or 5 feet per mile were maintained throughout its entire course, Current River would not be a particularly interesting or exciting stream to navigate by canoe or John-boat. But be-

cause of the cutting action of the water along the river bed and the varying densities of the rocks through which it must work its way, this even fall is not maintained. Instead, the stream proceeds in a series of pools which flow placidly beneath high limestone bluffs and which alternate with swift, snag-filled "chutes" or boulder-strewn rapids where the drop may be several feet in a distance of a few hundred yards.

In times of normal water there is enough current flowing through most of the pools to make hard paddling unnecessary, and, though few of the rapids are dangerous for the experienced boatman, they are swift enough to require quick thinking and a considerable knowledge of the stream. They send the canoe rushing down a lane of dancing whitecaps, with vigorous paddling necessary where the current plunges at right angles through overhanging limbs into the rocky bank. Many a novice, piloting his craft down Current River or Jacks Fork for the first time and unfamiliar with the power of the water and the twists and turns of the channel, manages to swamp his craft a half-dozen times in a day's journey and is lucky to save his camp gear. By the same token, the experienced riverman may run these streams for a dozen years with never an accident.

Only during recent years has Current River been brought into easy reach of the recreationist through the building of a good state highway system. Up until the time this happened, the stream offered perhaps the finest smallmouth-bass fishing in the United States. Increased fishing pressure brought about by the larger number of fishermen has affected this reputation to some extent; yet it is to the credit of the American sportsman that hundreds come back season after season

as much for the incomparable beauty of this Ozark river as for the fishing. The "float trip"—with boats, provisions, and guides furnished by one of the outfitters in the small towns on the watershed—is in the nature of an annual pilgrimage.

For the outdoorsman who dispenses with guides—who brings his own canoe and camp gear and provisions and pilots his own craft—Current River is as close to wilderness as anything the Midwest offers this side of the Quetico-Superior, up along the Canadian border. There are, as a matter of fact, only four highways which cross the stream on bridges in its 150-mile course. There are, in addition, two or three primitive ferries which use a cable and the force of the current for motive power. Since a fair day's float is fifteen miles, one can spend a week on the river going downstream and see little of civilization. The few natives one encounters along the bank meet friendliness with friendliness. Around each bend, a new gravel bar offers an attractive campsite. There is firewood aplenty from the big drifts piled up during times of flood. For the dedicated angler there is fishing enough, with always the chance of a really memorable day's sport.

There is, for the rest of us, beauty to be captured on film or in the mind's eye; birds and wildlife of many kinds; innumerable wildflowers, since the Ozarks boast a varied flora. Finally, there is that wonderful sensation of peace and relaxation that comes nowadays only when we leave the din and hurry of the city, the bustle of traffic on the highways—when for a space we shake off the trappings of civilization and take to the wilderness.

3 FROM THE BEGINNING

Whether a small and comparatively self-contained unit of land such as is embraced by the Current River watershed can be said to have a history depends on the point of view. If we define history in terms of vast movements of populations, the rise and fall of cultures and dynasties, the marching and countermarching of armies, then this small and isolated part of our continent's oldest mountains can hardly be said to have an important history. It has influenced the destiny of no civilization, seen no great historic battles; indeed, it might almost be said to have slept through countless eons.

If we think of history, on the other hand, in terms of any of a number of specialized fields of knowledge, then the Current River country has a story to tell. For the geologist, paleontologist, archeologist, biologist, ecologist—even for the sociologist—the area provides a rich mine of interesting material. The scientist in any of these disciplines could write his own book about the region on his own particular subject.

The Geological Background

Beginnings are likely to be lost in the dimness of time, and this is true of the beginnings of the Ozark highland. Yet we can trace the geologic history of Current River back to the pre-Cambrian period generally referred to as Algonkian. This was the time dur-

ing which the rhyolite porphyry that today forms the "basement" structure of the Ozarks was extruded through a still older surface during a long period of igneous activity caused by the earth's internal fires. It is hardly possible to determine the exact extent of Algonkian time, although it is generally agreed to have ended some 550 million years ago and to have occupied a period at least as long as all those which have succeeded it. No fossils have survived from the Algonkian, although carbon deposits in some of the "prehistoric" rocks indicate that life did exist during this period and that it was fairly abundant. Heat and pressure through the ages, however, combined to destroy whatever fossil record existed.

The story of the Ozark highland during the next 300 million years can be charted as one of uplift, erosion, submergence beneath salt-water seas, and receding waters followed by emergence, uplift, and erosion again. Two ocean inundations occurred early during the Cambrian period that ended 475 million years ago; and each inundation left its record in layers of sandstone and dolomite limestone and shale deposited on the floor of that particular ocean. These earliest limestones are called the Bonne Terre and Potosi and contain almost no fossils except for a rarely discovered trilobite and gastropod. There is evidence that as the ocean receded after the second submergence, the Ozark region was the last on our continent to appear above water.

Once again during late Cambrian time the sea covered the Current River country, and in the deep layer of Eminence limestone deposited during this inundation there appears a rich store of fossils, which now includes both fauna and flora. Among the former, in ad-

dition to trilobites and gastropods, are many brachiopods; while plants are represented by the algae called Cryptozoa. All of this fossil life appears in three distinct zones, indicating that this inundation lasted a very long time.

In the Ordovician period that followed the Cambrian and embraced some 175 million years, there were two more submergences which left their record in the limestone layers of the Current River country; and one of these was definitely tropical in character. Then in late Ordovician, Mississipian, and Pennsylvanian time, which lasted about 100 million years and ended 200 million years ago, there are evidences of five more submergences of the Ozark area. But here, except for traces, the limestones have entirely dissolved or eroded away, and the only remaining record lies in deposits of residual cherts and flints left in the lowest parts of the basins. These rocks, being almost insoluble, have defied dissolution.

Even the older limestones are not, of course, present over the entire Ozark highland; for these were subjected to long periods of erosion during times of uplift or when the ocean waters had receded. There are areas where all of these layers have dissolved away, to expose knobs and peaks of igneous rock; yet in other areas they are buried deep beneath later formations in the lower basins of the mountains. Often the underlying layers were exposed by faulting—sometimes by the downward cutting of a river—and here the overlapping formations can be readily seen and studied.

There is no evidence of submergence of the Current River country or any of the Ozark highland since the end of the Pennsylvanian period some 200 million years

ago. Uplift and erosion, however, went steadily on, wearing the mountains down into a fairly level plain and then pushing them upward again. This process continued until comparatively recent time—as the geologist reckons time—probably ending early during the Pliocene period that occupied the last 25 million years up to the beginning of the Pleistocene, a mere million years ago. We know this because Current River and other streams of the region are still cutting downward through the rock, and, even though some have begun to develop narrow flood plains, none has as yet reached grade.

The Current River watershed, having been both dry land and ocean bed many times during its long geologic history, undoubtedly saw the appearance and gradual disappearance of vast numbers of life forms which evolved and developed on many parts of our planet. Scientists still differ in the naming and exact dating of geologic periods, so that I have here for convenience collapsed Silurian and Devonian time into the Ordovician period. The fossil record is so clear, however, that there is little disagreement among paleontologists as to the general order in which life forms developed.

Not much is known of the Algonkian period, although it is inferred that life existed, perhaps in the form of simple invertebrates and some predecessor of the algae. Cambrian time brings the first clear record of life in marine fossils which include the major groups of invertebrates and algae. In the Ordovician period as used here, the first vertebrates evolved and the first known life appeared on land. Insects and land plants came into being, while fish dominated the seas and some became amphibians. Mississippian and Pennsylvanian time are

known as the "carboniferous" period, when vast forested swamps of coal-forming tree ferns covered large areas of the planet. This included much of the Ozark highland.

All this development and change the Current River country experienced. Since that time 200 million years ago, however, it has stood somewhat aloof, rearing its rugged shoulders above successive invasions by the sea that covered large parts of the continent. It watched the birth of newer mountain ranges—the southern Appalachians, Sierra Nevadas, Rockies, and the western coastal range that is probably still in process of formation. During these millennia the Ozark highland saw the final extinction of whole groups of plants and animals as these failed to meet the challenge of a changing environment. It saw the birth and development of primitive and then modern conifers and seed plants. It stood below the farthest advance of the glaciers, although it must have experienced far-reaching changes in fauna and flora because of changing climate during this period.

As might be expected of so old a region, the Ozark highland during modern geologic time developed soils of considerable complexity; these being fed by the underlying limestones made up of the skeletons of ancient life forms and fed also by the deposit of organic matter from the bodies of countless generations of plants and animals during the long ages. During modern geologic time—which is to say, the last few hundred thousand years—a rich plant and animal life evolved or invaded the Ozark highland and became adapted there.

This complex of modern fauna and flora, which included 2,000 species of plants and 700 of higher animals,

remained largely stable and in equilibrium until a few geologic seconds ago, when the Ozarks were invaded by "civilized" man. Then, in a period of no more than 200 years, much that had been accomplished by Nature in the preceding millions of years was undone. The history of this period of civilized man's occupation of the Ozarks makes a fascinating study for the ecologist, whose interest is in the relationships between living forms and their environments. The region is also of considerable interest to the botanist and zoologist because of its plant and animal life.

The Coming of Man

Compared with geologic history, or with even that of various plant and animal forms, the story of man in the Ozark highland occupies no more than an instant in time. Nor did early man, so far as we can determine, have much more effect on the over-all environment than the wild creatures which roamed the forests and high prairies. Near Current River, the earliest men of whom we have record—and this record is still somewhat meager—were mound builders. Their greatest concentrations were, naturally, along the broad alluvial valley of the Mississippi, for they were agricultural people and little skilled in the arts of war even as carried on in primitive societies. They lived in villages of considerable size, were potters and weavers, and counted the slingshot among their weapons. This device, incidentally, was unknown to later Indians who followed the mound builders in the region.

There were at least two—and perhaps three or four —types of mound-building cultures. The earliest were

the Bluff Dwellers, who made their homes in limestone caves and were skilled artists, although they had not discovered the use of bow and arrow. The Woodland culture, which apparently inhabited the smaller river valleys, also seems somewhat more primitive than the Mississippian. Their pottery was simpler, their grave mounds smaller, and their arrow points and stone tools were roughly chipped. The mounds of the Mississippian builders are more elaborate and larger, their pottery shows a higher degree of form and artistry, and their tools and implements of war and the hunt are finely made.

Whether the cultures of the mound builders existed together, overlapped, or succeeded each other is difficult to determine today. Certainly, however, they continued in the Ozark highland for a period of many centuries. It was originally believed that these people might have been related to pre-Aztec or Toltec types found in Mexico and that they were eventually overrun and exterminated by the Indians of historic times. Recently, however, accumulating evidence about the crafts, burial customs, and traditions of the later Indians points to a close cultural relationship with the prehistoric peoples. To try to re-create the lives of the mound builders would be tantamount to writing fiction, which is not the purpose of this book; so we will leave them for the "historic" Indians about whom more is known.

Although a number of tribes in their wanderings touched the Ozark highland and the Current River country between the time of Hernando de Soto and the extinction of the last Indian land titles in the early 1800's, there seems no doubt that the Osages were dom-

inant here during a period of several hundred years. Historians who accompanied the earliest Spanish explorers drew such a long bow in their reporting and mixed so much imagination with fact, however, that all their accounts must be taken with a large grain of salt.

The almost incredible march that brought De Soto and his adventurous followers to Missouri was inspired by their predecessor, the equally incredible Cabeza de Vaca. This amazing character, shipwrecked on the west coast of Florida in 1528, had spent eight years walking across almost the entire breadth of the North American continent and eventually arrived in Mexico City, which was already a stronghold of the Spaniards. The account that De Vaca brought back of a vast unexplored territory to the north set off a new wave of excitement in Spain. Hernando de Soto, a follower of Pizarro with some years of experience in the New World, received permission to organize an expedition of conquest into the American Southwest. His reputation was such that he had no difficulty in raising an army of 600 cavalry and infantry and in outfitting these adventurers for the long journey ahead.

Since our purpose here is only to document the evidence of De Soto's penetration of the boundaries of present-day Missouri, no attempt will be made to detail his battles and adventures on the march from the Bay of Tampa through the present Gulf States to the Mississippi River. We know, however, that he left Tampa Bay about May 30, 1539, and finally arrived at a point on the Mississippi, probably between the mouths of the Arkansas and St. Francis, whence he crossed to the west bank to continue his explorations.

There were three chroniclers of the De Soto expedi-

tion, and by carefully sifting and matching up their accounts, historians have been able to trace his route with fair accuracy. The chief chronicler, Garcilasso de Vega, was not actually present but wrote his history by interviewing as many as possible of the survivors. Another account published in 1557 and signed "Gentleman of Elvas" was evidently the work of a member of De Soto's band, as was a much shorter narrative written by Louis Fernandez Biedma and published in 1544. Since there is general agreement as to Indian tribes met and types of landscape traversed, there seems little reason to doubt that De Soto and his band were the first white men to visit the Ozark region.

The route followed by the army after crossing the Mississippi led northward up the long tongue of high land known as Crowley's Ridge, which runs from present-day Arkansas into Missouri. This ridge follows roughly the east bank of the St. Francis River, separating it from the broad flood plain of the Mississippi. The Indian tribes encountered by De Soto and his men can be identified as the Kaskaskias, Quapaws, Arkansas, and Osages, who existed, it would seem, in a perpetual state of intermittent warfare. With some of these, the Spaniards managed to establish peaceful relations, even gaining allies for their conquest of other tribes. Food in the rich delta country was fairly plentiful, for the chroniclers report fields of maize, fruits of many kinds, nuts and vegetables. In one battle which drove the Quapaws from a principal village, a rich store of skins and hides of deer, buffalo, panther, bear, and bobcat enabled the ragged army to replenish its moccasins and wearing apparel.

As De Soto moved north and west, side expeditions

were sent out, and one of these is reported to have returned with a considerable amount of copper ore. Always, however, the gold lay just ahead. When one studies the history of the fairly well-defined Indian trails which traversed this countryside and matches these up with the descriptions of the chroniclers, its seems fairly certain that the Spaniards touched lower Current River somewhere in the neighborhood of the present-day town of Doniphan and then reached their "farthest north" among the granitic knobs of the St. Francois Mountains in what is now Iron County. From here the army turned southwest, following rumors that the gold lay in that direction.

If De Soto again followed the "Indian highways," as seems likely, he must have crossed the headwaters of the Current and moved thence into the White River country and the Boston Mountains of Arkansas. The westernmost point touched by the expedition was somewhere in eastern Oklahoma. There the army turned back, still hearing rumors of gold ahead but unable to proceed farther. Their leader, however, was fated not to see Spain again, for somewhere along the banks of the lower Mississippi he died and was buried in its muddy waters.

The evidence that the great conquistador and explorer Don Francesco Vasquez de Coronado reached the Ozark country is more tenuous than that on which De Soto's claims are based. Yet certain aspects of it seem worth presenting. Coronado's expedition, like that of De Soto, was inspired by the accounts of the legendary De Vaca. His army was gathered at Compostela on the far shores of the Pacific in northwest Mexico and the purpose of its march was to discover

and conquer the golden "Seven Cities of Cibola" which De Vaca had reported. The expedition set out in February of 1540, only a few months after De Soto's departure from Tampa Bay; but, although he was equally unsuccessful in finding gold, Coronado at least made it back safely to his starting point. The Seven Cities turned out to be no more than the pueblos of the Zuni Indians in the bleak Arizona desert and were quite devoid of treasure.

As always, however, there were rumors of gold to eastward, and this was enough to whet the insatiable appetite of the Spaniards. The full story of Coronado's march need not be detailed here, although its course has been traced along the Rio Grande, across the Pecos and the Canadian, and through a vast expanse of buffalo country. Toward the end of his eastward journey, Coronado left the army and pushed ahead with a small band of followers to find Quivira, a city reported by an Indian guide to contain much treasure.

From this point, both Coronado and the chroniclers who accompanied him seem to agree that they traveled northeastward until they found mountains, which could only have been the Ozarks. They marched through a land of many streams, and that could hardly have been Oklahoma or Kansas or even the prairie country of western Missouri. They also encountered the Osage Indians whom Coronado describes accurately in his letters to the king of Spain.

One unusually intelligent reporter and member of the expedition, Captain Jaramillo, states that on the bank of a great river, just before they turned west to start the long journey back to Mexico, they planted a cross bearing the words "Francesco Vasquez de Coro-

nado, General of the Army, arrived here." The river could have been the Mississippi. With one more bit of information we will leave the Ozark country to the Indians again for a period of 200 years. Some historians believe that in July or August of 1541 the bands of De Soto and Coronado must have been camped in this region within a few days march of each other. Some rumor of De Soto's presence apparently reached Coronado, who sent an Indian runner out with letters. The runner was unable to find De Soto's force, and the messages went undelivered. It is interesting to speculate, at least, that the camps of the two intrepid leaders may have been located in the rugged Ozark highland as De Soto headed southwest while Coronado was still marching to the northeast. What seems certain is that De Soto actually traversed the country that lies along Current River watershed and that Coronado also saw this rugged wilderness, whether or not he marched across it and camped on the banks of the stream.

The Spaniards were indefatigable explorers, rugged and without fear and ever ready to push out into the unknown when some rumor of riches reached them. Since they were well established at Natchitoches in the early 1700's, it seems probable that between this date and the time of De Soto, 150 years earlier, the Ozarks were penetrated by more than one small band, the story of whose wanderings has been lost to history. At any rate, the next penetration of the region of which we have historical record was made by the French who traveled southward along the course of the Mississippi.

These early French explorers were as tough and courageous as the Spaniards, and there is evidence that they were even better woodsmen. Moreover, since the

purpose of the Spaniards was to find existing although perhaps hidden stores of gold and silver, the survival of the Indians was of no importance to them; and whenever they moved or settled down in strength, this fact governed their attitude toward the native population. If it was useful to provide labor, it survived. If not, it was wiped out. The French, on the other hand, operated from a different and double motive. One part of this was to convert the heathen savage, a labor which the Jesuit fathers pursued in the face of incredible hardship. The other was to develop trade with the Indians, chiefly for the rich store of furs which this wilderness possessed.

The first French explorations along the Mississippi into the borders of what is now Missouri came from the north by way of the Great Lakes, and the names of many of the early travelers are well known to history. First of all, perhaps, were the traders Radisson and Groseilliers, who made several trips down the great river between 1650 and 1665. These two wilderness travelers worked intermittently for the British and French, as served their immediate interests, and founded the Hudson Bay Company in 1670. Others even better known are Marquette and Menard, Joliet, La Salle, and Cadillac. Thus the Mississippi and the lands adjoining it were opened up by French coming from the north, rather than Spaniards from the south, and in 1682 La Salle, arriving at the mouth of the Mississippi, claimed the entire valley for France and named it Louisiana in honor of his king.

It appears that only Radisson and Groseilliers, of the early explorers, traveled much afield from the banks of the Mississippi. But close on their heels came the *couriers des bois*, those intrepid "runners of the woods"

who penetrated all the wilderness of Canada as well as that lying west of the Mississippi. It was these men, trappers and small traders with the Indian tribes, who gave the Current its first and most appropriate name —*La Riviere Courante,* or "Running River."

Not only the stream but the region itself was named by these woodsmen; or, at least, no other way has been found to account for the word "Ozarks." It is said on the best available authority that all the mountainous area lying to the south and west of Ste. Genevieve, Fort Chartres, and St. Louis was known to the early French as "the country of the Arkansas," which referred in a general way to the Indian tribes living there. When a trapper heading out to the south or southwest was asked where he was going, he answered, "Aux Arkansas." This was abbreviated to *aux Arks* and finally Anglicized by the American settlers to "Ozarks."

French miners and then settlers followed on the heels of the trappers, traders, and missionaries. Old Jesuit journals show that by 1700 there was lead being mined in the Meramec River country of the northern Ozarks. By 1735 a permanent settlement had been established at Ste. Genevieve on the banks of the Mississippi, and this was soon followed by Mine au Breton (now Potosi) some 50 miles inland, then by others. By this time the rivers of the Ozarks were beginning to yield their treasure of furs, and the region had been explored by Du Tisne, who opened up trade with the Osages.

The Osages were an outstanding people. This is agreed by all explorers and travelers through the Ozark highland with the exception of the Calvinist missionaries who came along in the early decades of the nineteenth century and in the case of the single historian

Brackenridge. Among the others, there is general agreement that the men of the Osage tribe were of remarkable height, few being less than six feet tall. "Well-formed, athletic and robust men of noble aspect," was Audubon's comment; and the famed ornithologist had met many tribes of Indians. Another naturalist, Nutall, says, "The activity and agility of the Osages is scarcely credible. They will not uncommonly walk from their villages to the trading houses, a distance of sixty miles, in a day."

Zebulon Pike reports meeting the chief of the Little Osages, Whetstone, who had marched with the French to attack Detroit and been present at the defeat of Braddock as he came westward from the Cumberland Mountains to attack Fort Duquesne. With Whetstone were "all the warriors who could be spared from his villages." The Osages were absent seven months on this expedition, which must have involved a march of 3,000 miles and attests to their tremendous vitality. Stephen Long, Sibley, and other competent military observers agree that the Osages were distinguished for sobriety and intelligence, for some knowledge of such sciences as medicine and astronomy, for sharing the spoils of the hunt among their lodges, and for the care expended on their children and on the aged and invalid members of their bands.

Although surrounded on every side by hostile tribes, many of whom received firearms from the whites long before they did, the Osages maintained themselves masters of the Ozark highland. Their numbers, despite continuous warfare and the vicissitudes of wilderness life, remained constant and close to the carrying capacity of the region. In summer they hunted the buffalo

and elk on the high bluestem prairies and in winter found refuge in narrow valleys such as the one along Current River, which knew many of their villages. In permanent settlements they erected pole lodges of considerable size, these being walled and roofed with woven mats which were quite waterproof. When hunting, they raised shelters of buffalo hide.

In addition to hunting, the Osages planted annual crops of corn, beans, squash, and pumpkins. And although the cycle of the year was often interrupted by war, raids, and trading expeditions, it went something like this: Crops were planted in April, after which the Indians left for the summer buffalo hunt and returned in August for the harvest. After a season of feasting at the lodges, the remaining food was cached, and each band set out in September on the autumn hunt which lasted normally until about Christmas. Then again came a time of feasting and leisure in the villages which lasted until March, when the tribe set out to hunt bear and take the annual harvest of beaver pelts. In addition to wild game and their simple crops, the Osages collected and stored such foods of the forest as walnuts and hickory nuts, pecans, hazelnuts and chinquipin acorns, grapes, plums, papaws, persimmons, and wild edible roots. All these were gathered in season and preserved with care.

The dress of the Osage warrior consisted of moccasins, soft-tanned deerskin leggings that came almost to the thigh, breechclout of colored cloth, and buckskin hunting shirt pulled over the head or a buffalo robe thrown about the shoulders. The chief weapon was the bow, in the use of which the warriors were remarkably proficient; and this was supplemented on oc-

casion by war club, knife, tomahawk, and spear. From the time when they were first reported by De Soto's chronicler, the men of the Osage tribe shaved their heads clean except for a long scalplock that stood high in the air and was often decorated, making them seem even taller than they were.

The Osage women wore their hair long and parted in the middle. Leggings were of bright cloth, shorter than those of the men and often with a fringe on the outer edge. A square of cloth fastened on the hip made a short skirt, and another was thrown over the shoulders, although this was often laid aside in hot weather. Ornaments and decorations of beads, brass, or silver were worn, and tattooing was common among the Osages as with most Indian tribes. Babies were carried on the papoose board, and during summer the children went naked.

As white settlers invaded the Osage country, trapping became a primary occupation of the warriors; and Current River contributed its share of pelts of beaver, mink, and otter. Deer hides were a standard trade item, although by this time the buffalo and elk had disappeared from the Ozark highland. The relationship between the Osages and the invading whites was remarkably good and generally peaceful. The Indians were not above stealing horses and an occasional cow from the settlers. This was, however, no more than long-established custom, like raiding against neighboring tribes.

In addition to the encroachment of the whites, there was steady pressure on the Osages from Indian tribes to north and west who were themselves being displaced by the westward march of the frontier. First to cross the Mississippi, pushed by the Americans and

welcomed by the Spaniards, were the Shawnee and Delaware bands who built their villages on the eastern edge of the Ozark escarpment and were, in their turn, pushed westward into the mountains. The Cherokees from the southern Appalachians came next, the first bands settling along the streams of the eastern Ozarks not long after the Revolutionary War.

In the years following the Louisiana Purchase, one treaty after another pushed the Osages westward until by 1825 their last land titles within the boundaries of Missouri had been extinguished. Then between 1832 and 1836 the land claims of Shawnee, Delaware, Sauk and Fox were ended, and all the tribes had moved westward. An epoch in the history of the Current River country had ended.

The first American settlers who came into the newly acquired lands that now embrace Missouri were, for the most part, of British stock. Not all of them, however, were alike. Farmers from the Piedmont and Shenandoah and from the Bluegrass region of Tennessee and Kentucky came with their slaves and took up land in the alluvial valleys of the Missouri and Mississippi. A scattering of families from Pennsylvania, Ohio, New York, and New England pushed westward onto the unbroken prairie.

The people who settled the rugged valleys of the southern Ozarks were different. They came out of the mountain country of Tennessee, Kentucky, West Virginia, and Pennsylvania. They were hunters and frontiersmen by nature and three generations of environment—granted that some of them mined intermittently, logged when it suited them, ran a few cattle and hogs in the forest, and raised the smallest possible number of

acres of corn and garden crops. Schoolcraft, writing of the region in 1818, states that "furs and peltries are taken down the river at certain seasons in canoes and disposed of to traders who visit the lower river. Here they receive in exchange for their furs, woolen clothes, rifles, knives, salt, powder and lead." In writing of these people, the ecologist Fraser Darling recently pointed out that their ancestors who left the British Isles in the 1600's and 1700's were chiefly recruited from among forest dwellers, poachers, charcoal burners, and the like, so that they came naturally by their ability as woodsmen, spirit of utter independence, and disregard for authority as represented by game laws, grazing regulations, and absentee ownership of timber.

The scarcity of human population and the abundance of game made the Current River country ideal for the life these people liked to lead. One early traveler, Featherstonhaugh, said that in the early 1800's "the country abounded in millions of deer, turkeys, bear, wolves and small animals. I remember, as my father moved west, that we could see deer feeding in great herds on the hills like cattle and wild turkeys were in abundance. Wild meat was so plentiful that early settlers subsisted on it. Bees abounded and were hunted for beeswax, while furs and hides constituted the currency of the country."

Although there are few written records of the history of the region, it seems clear from the evidence we can gather that man's impact on the Ozark landscape was so slight as to be hardly noticeable until the second half of the nineteenth century. The Indian tribes lived by maintaining themselves in balance with the environment, having little more effect upon it than the herds of

deer in the forest. Only in burning the prairie during the buffalo drive did they alter the natural scene—although lightning fires might have accomplished this same result.

The Spaniards were transients in the Ozark highland. They appeared for a moment in history and were gone. The effect of the French was hardly greater than that of the Spaniards. A few more of them came, and some of these remained as settlers, but in small and isolated communities. Their mining and farming activities were of limited scope, although the same could hardly be said for hunting and trapping which doubtless began the depletion of the game herds and furbearers and put considerable pressure on the Indian tribes who depended upon these for food, clothing, and commerce.

Land Going Downhill

The American settlers who came to the mountain country of Missouri prior to the Civil War had somewhat more effect on the land than did the Indians, Spaniards, or French trappers and traders. They lived in much the same way, depending upon the forests and streams for food and for the peltries that served as currency. Unlike the Indians and the French, however, these American settlers stayed longer in one place. Thus they killed out the game species and in a very few years had displaced the Indian tribes entirely. And even though these frontiersmen sometimes moved on, it was generally not until considerable damage had been done to the wilderness.

Serious retrogression of the Ozark environment, however, began in the years that followed the Civil War and

in many areas has continued until today. During the war, lawless bands of bushwhackers found refuge in the rough river hills and lived by attacking the scattered settlements and outlying farmsteads, so that some of the better people were driven out. When the war ended, there was a considerable influx of home-seeking families of small means who were encouraged by the Homestead Act of 1862 and who took up farming on lands ill suited to the purpose. Their stock summered in the forest and wintered on starvation rations of wild hay and a little grain raised by the settlers.

This kind of farming could go on where homesteads occupied the stream valleys or better limestone uplands, though the livestock load was becoming too heavy for the limited carrying capacity of the woodland range. Even then, the Ozark razorback hog (which is no character of fiction) became famous. Cows averaged 375 pounds in weight, and it was a mighty 4-year-old steer that tipped the scales at 500 pounds. Moreover, as the livestock load increased, the quality of the forage declined. Nuritious, drought-resistant grasses such as the big and little bluestem and Indian and plumegrass were killed out, as were many of the native legumes. Their places were taken on the small prairies and in forest glades and openings by brush and sprouts of weed trees such as blackjack oak and sassafras. Only such unpalatable grasses as broom sedge and annual cheat survived overgrazing.

The Ozark livestock farmer somehow got the idea that this situation was caused by the annual layer of litter on the forest floor. Burn it up! he resolved, and thus began the custom of "burning the woods to make

the grass grow," which, more than any other practice, has harmed the Ozark timberlands.

Logging in the Ozark forests began first on the watersheds of streams that flowed toward St. Louis, the largest lumber market. But by the end of the Civil War, the cream had been skimmed from this region, and the lumbermen had moved into the Current River country. As logging progressed, large sawmill settlements grew up, the mills at Grandin and West Eminence being rated for some years as the largest in the nation. This attracted a large population of additional workers into the country; and many of these, when they were left stranded by the eventual closing of the mills, were forced into submarginal farming on the steep mountainsides and into small logging and sawmilling operations which were—and are—equally marginal. The last of the virgin pine and oak finally disappeared from the deepest and roughest hollows.

All in all, the picture of land use in the Current River country for the past hundred years has not been a happy one. It has been largely a picture of land going downhill. Over-logging, overgrazing, poor farming, and erosion have combined to seriously reduce the life-carrying capacity of the region. As the good timber and forage plants disappeared, their places were taken by others less commercially valuable and less palatable. Wildlife largely disappeared, and fewer game fish grew in gravel-choked streams. This is Nature's only means for healing a ruined landscape and is the means she always adopts when her resources are ruthlessly overexploited.

There are some signs today that things are on the

mend. On the whole, the human population of the southern Ozarks is declining, and this is, for the time being, a good thing. More and more citizens of the region are coming to understand what has happened here in the past hundred years—and what steps must be taken in a program of rehabilitation. If these eventually win out over the selfish minority who would continue to overexploit the dwindling resources, there is a future ahead for the Current River country. Forest-land owner, livestock farmer, and recreationist will all share in this future.

4 CROSS SECTION

Since Ginnie's and my interest in the Montauk Springs country which forms the headwaters of Current River lies chiefly in its scenic beauty, we like best to go there in late April or early May, when the Ozark wildflowers make their finest display. The trip is not an arduous one, for Montauk is located only seventy-five miles to the west of our farm, Possum Trot, and we can drive the distance over good roads in two hours with no difficulty. This is a far cry from expeditions we used to make thirty years ago. Then, we were fortunate if we spent no more than two hours on the last fifteen miles. It is even farther from the days when the earliest settlers, who came to Current River valley in the 1830's, made one journey each year to Rolla by ox team to do their trading. The round-trip distance was 120 miles, and it normally took three weeks.

The best time to go to Montauk is in mid-week. The area surrounding the big springs has been developed into an attractive State Park with a hatchery for rainbow trout and several miles of fast, cold fishing water. Anglers come from all parts of Missouri to cast for trout during the season, but only on weekends are there likely to be enough of them on hand so that accommodations cannot be secured at the comfortable cottages or space found on the campgrounds. During mid-week, except at the opening of the trout season, the area is uncrowded and retains much of the charm it possessed as wilderness.

Our route from Possum Trot Farm to Montauk lies for the first fifty miles across Highway 32 to Salem, seat of government for Dent County. This road traverses such a typical cross section of Ozark countryside that it seems worth describing. After leaving our farm in Belleview Valley we climb the western rim of the St. Francois Mountains, oldest of all the Ozark ranges. The floor of the valley is good farmland, laid down on an ancient limestone bed. The mountains themselves, subjected to erosion through the centuries, have worn down to the igneous rock and today present to the sky their granite crests, sparsely covered with forest vegetation.

Once past the rim of these hills, which extend westward for a dozen miles, the road comes out on one of those fairly level, plateau-like uplands that occur intermittently throughout the Ozark highland. These generally mark a "height of land" between watersheds, and the one extending from the St. Francois Mountains westward is no exception. It is, in fact, the backbone of the entire Ozark range, separating the northern from the southern escarpment. On the right as one travels westward are headwaters of the streams that flow north to the Missouri or enter the Mississippi in the neighborhood of St. Louis. On the left are the little creeks that flow south and eventually join to form the Black and Current Rivers, finally reaching the Mississippi via White River, far down in Arkansas.

As might be supposed, the thin and granitic soils of the St. Francois hills create little arable land except in narrow alluvial valleys along the creeks. Nor do they provide the best environment for forest growth, as compared with deeper and less eroded Ozark soils.

Once the plateau is reached, however, conditions for tree growth improve; and I like to picture this land as it was when it was true wilderness—before the white man came.

Forest to Pasture to Desert

We know that in this not-so-far-off time it was a common thing for migrating herds of buffalo to traverse the Ozark country, grazing eastward to the banks of the Mississippi, while bands of elk found the forest openings to their liking. Whitetail deer inhabited this vast woodland in large numbers, and fleet-footed antelope used the open glades and limestone prairies which were covered with bluestem grass. Great flocks of wild turkeys harvested the acorn crop; ruffed grouse drummed in the deep woods; and, during the mating season, the booming of the prairie chicken sounded at dawn from every glade. Furbearers were plentiful—black bear and raccoon in the forest and beaver, mink, and otter in every stream. Often during migration it took many hours for the armies of gray squirrels to cross a river. Timber and brush wolves, as well as bobcat and panther, took their toll; yet they did no more than keep the numbers of their prey in balance with the carrying capacity of the range.

The human inhabitants of these hills and valleys, the Osage Indians, lived of course in a Stone Age. And while this has no bearing on their intelligence, which was high, it is no wonder they were unable to stand against the gun and plow of the white settler. The Osage was primarily a food gatherer and not a husbandman. The deer and elk and buffalo were his cattle;

his crops were the fruits and nuts and wild plants of the forest and prairie. He knew the uses of root and leaf and bark for food and medicine, uses which are largely forgotten today.

This culture of the Indian of the plains and woods was diametrically opposed to that of the European settler who displaced him. It was based on an existence lived in harmony with Nature—on a skilful adaptation to the existing environment and an instinctively maintained equilibrium with all of the elements which made up this environment. It depended for success upon the preservation in an unimpaired state of its natural resources. If deer or buffalo grew scarce, the Indian moved his abode and the depleted herds recovered. The food chain, reduced to its simplest equation, might be stated as acorn-deer-Indian. The white man inherited from the Indian an unspoiled, virgin land. What he did with it is something to think about! Suffice it to say here that the change was to a philosophy and practice of domestic husbandry based chiefly upon exotic species and ruthless exploitation of every natural resource for immediate profit.

The virgin forest at that time covered some 30 million acres of the Ozark landscape and consisted primarily of hardwoods, with occasional mixed or pure stands of short-leaf pine. Since pine is fast growing and is today readily salable, considerable study has been given to its natural range, which is estimated to have covered approximately 5 million acres in the Ozarks. Of the hardwoods, scarlet oak of the black-oak family was probably the dominant species, with fairly extensive stands of the slower growing white oak, as well as black and red oak, post oak, and blackjack. Hickory and sour

gum also grew on the steep slopes, while alluvial valleys supported good stands of walnut and hard maple.

The history of forest use in the Ozarks could hardly be demonstrated better than in the plateau area lying along Highway 32 between Possum Trot Farm and Salem. The first serious commercial timber cutting was done here in the late 1800's, and the method followed was what we know today as "high-grading." This simply means that the best and most easily marketed trees were taken first, without regard to damage to the remaining timber, tree reproduction, or any other consideration except to skim the cream for the quickest profit. Thus the readily salable pine was logged off and then, in successive waves of cutting, the various species of oak.

Little or no attention was paid in those times to trees with less commercial value, although eventually the walnut was harvested and then the hickory, which was used for farm-tool handles and wagon parts. In this particular area of the Ozarks, which was neither very rugged nor far from market, the remaining tree growth was now slashed clean to make charcoal. If this had been the end, the forest would somehow have started making a comeback. But the hill people looked at this cut-over land, no longer useful to the lumberman, and decided it would make pasture for their livestock. As the first step toward putting it to this use, they set fire to it, in the mistaken belief that this would permanently keep down the brushy second-growth trees and also make the grass grow. And for a short time this is what actually happened, since the ash from the burning slashes created a certain amount of available plant food. Some grass grew; most of this being short-lived

annual species with low nutritive value which furnished, at best, a few weeks of poor grazing in early summer.

The long-range result of this treatment of the land, which included annual burning and grazing by far more cattle, goats, hogs, and horses than the range could carry, was disastrous; as it has been throughout history and on every continent. A deep layer of humus is created in a forest by decaying matter and by the annual fall of leaves. On the burned-out land this of course soon disappeared. The thin topsoil washed away down the hollows until there was little left but rocky chert, and the mountain streams became choked with gravel. Trampling feet of sharp-hoofed animals compacted the soil to speed still further the run-off from every rain. Now almost no water seeped into the earth to feed springs, streams, and the permanent underground reservoir. The cut-over forest lands of the Ozarks became, for all practical purposes, a biological desert. Starting with the soil fauna and flora which are essential to the processes of both growth and decay of plants, the land supported steadily less life. Game birds and wild animals disappeared because of lack of food and cover; and the fish population in every stream declined for the same reason. But still the hill folk burned each spring, then turned out their thin animals to forage, until the Ozarks became one of the depressed rural areas of America.

It was in 1936 or thereabouts that the U. S. Forest Service, which had been recently authorized to acquire land in Missouri, took over some of this land to create the 1,600,000-acre Missouri National Forests. Fire protection was at once established and a combination program of education and enforcement was begun among

the hill people. Limits were set as to the numbers of livestock that could be grazed on National Forest lands. A small amount of pine planting was done on good sites during the CCC days; yet for the area as a whole it was found that planting was both uneconomic and largely unnecessary. Here and there an old gnarled pine or oak made seed and scattered it across the forest floor in years favorable to tree reproduction. No longer threatened by fire and the hungry mouths of livestock, the seedlings throve and grew. Slowly but surely the protected forest areas began to build back.

Much of the initial tree reproduction, it is true, was of blackjack oak and other inferior species having little commercial value. But the humus started to build up on the forest floor again, and here and there the seedlings of longer-lived and more valuable trees came through and survived. There were also, on the better sites, stands of young oak and pine that needed only protection to start growing. As often as possible, these were "released" by girdling the old diseased and cull trees, salvaging any that could be used for lumber, and cutting down the undesirable brushy species. All of this work returned huge quantities of organic matter to the forest floor, and soon the rate of growth on the remaining oak and pine had doubled. Moreover, as organic matter in the soil increased, so did water absorption, for the rain no longer went rushing unimpeded down the hollows.

As we drive westward across Highway 32 through this National Forest land, we can see all these things beginning to happen, even though this is far from being one of the good sites for potential timber growth in the Ozarks. The day of profitable tree harvest is still some

years away; yet this day will surely come, as it already has in other parts of the Missouri National Forests where conditions were not so bad to begin with.

On the whole, however, the sort of bad land-use which I have described has been general throughout the entire Ozark hill country, differing only in degree. The pattern has been the same: successive waves of cutting with no thought of future growth or yield; fire deliberately set year after year in the attempt to create pasture; overgrazing by domestic animals; loss of humus and destruction of the topsoil; erosion and lack of ground-water storage; gravel siltation choking the larger rivers and gradual drying up of springs and smaller streams.

Conditions have improved tremendously during the past two decades on the land now held within the boundaries of our National Forests and on much smaller acreages of State land. But of the original 30 million acres of forest in the Ozark highland, only about 14 million acres now remain. Half, perhaps, of this remaining forest is today better protected through the extension of firefighting facilities. But on almost all privately owned land, protected against fire or not, timber management lags. This is especially true in the Ozark counties that still allow open-range grazing, where owners are under no obligation to keep their livestock within fences or on their own land. Since the value of timber on most cut-over Ozark land makes the cost of fencing altogether prohibitive, the open-range laws effectively defeat all attempts at good timber management. Yet the custom persists and will continue as long as regulatory power lies in the counties, where livestock owners always outnumber forest-land owners. The stockmen see

The Old Mill at Alley Spring

Current River Springs Run Cold and Clear

Float Fishing Can Be a Lazy Man's Sport

High Limestone Bluffs Border the Current River

Secretary Udall Inspects Ozark National Scenic
Riverways with the Author

Ozark Smallmouthed Bass Are Fighters

Contented Cooks Clean Up

A Good Jacks Fork Smallmouth

Jacks Fork Provides Missouri's Finest
Wilderness Canoe Water

Float Camp on a Breeze-Swept Gravel Bar

Big Spring Flows a Half-Billion Gallons a Day

On the Powder Mill Ferry

Comfortable Campgrounds Attract Visitors to State Parks

Crossing on the Powder Mill Ferry at Owls Bend

*Nature, Through Millions of Years,
Worked These Wonders . . .*

Man, in a Few Hours, Wrought This Desolation

The Ozark Scenic Riverways Conserve Nature's
Beauties for All

nothing wrong in exploiting and destroying the property of others.

As our highway nears the town of Salem, the land levels out still more, and much of it has been cleared for farming. It is not good cropland, the soil being both thin and gravelly, so that it suffers excessively during our normally dry Ozark summers. Yet under good management it produces moderately nutritive pasture and thus supports a considerable livestock industry. Out at the edges of the plateau where the land grows rougher, however, we are surprised at the large acreage which is being cleared for cultivation by the time-honored practice of "goating it off." The technique here is to girdle or chop the larger second-growth trees and then turn in flocks of goats, which are browsing animals. After these have eaten all the palatable shrubs and are at the point of starvation, they will tackle the less palatable species and finally, if kept hungry enough, will kill most of them out.

The odd thing about this rough land at the edges of the better farming country is that all of it has been cleared once and farmed to the point of abandonment by the original owner, a process which takes about a generation. Yet the minute this land will support a stand of sassafras sprouts and broom sedge—those infallible indicators of worn-out soil—someone gets the idea of farming it again, and the process of destruction starts all over. In fact, the goats often complete the cycle on this worn-out land before the farmer has a chance to make a crop. And still the custom of "goating off" the land refuses to die. It will survive, I suppose, until the last of the old settlers and many of their sons have passed to their reward. So we drive on toward

Montauk through the steeper hill country, hoping that when these old fellows reach the more fertile Elysian Fields on the other side of the Styx, they will cultivate them in a kindlier mood than they did these Ozark hills.

Trout and Orchids

Like most Ozark highways, the one which leads to Montauk Springs at the head of Current River follows for many miles a long and winding ridge. On either side the timbered hollows drop away steeply, and now in early May the hillsides are banked in graceful tiers of blossoming dogwood. The forest understory in Missouri boasts six members of this family, all of them attractive small trees bearing conspicuous clusters of white flowers. But it is *Cornus florida*, the white flowering dogwood, which blooms earliest and is the crowning glory of the Ozark spring.

The tree is at its best when it grows in the deeper, well-drained soils along the little creeks and spring branches; yet it thrives almost equally well on the rockiest hillsides, at the edges of clearings, and in the semishade of open timber. Its large, creamy white, four-petaled flowers normally appear ahead of the leaves and are doubly effective when seen against a background of redbud blossoms above the sparkling water of a mountain stream. Nor does the usefulness of *Cornus florida* end with its esthetic beauty; the wood is extremely hard, heavy, and close-grained, so that it is especially adapted to lathe-work and the manufacture of handles for small tools. Mountain people say the dogwood blooms twice, once in spring and again in autumn when it bears clusters of shining crimson

fruit which the birds harvest, while the leaves turn to brilliant red and tones of purple.

The flowering seasons of dogwood and redbud do not arrive simultaneously but, rather, overlap each other, with the redbud starting first. Thus the blossoms of *Cercis canadensis* which we see this late are on trees growing in favorably moist situations and in the deeper soils. Redbud, which also has the common name Judas tree, generally makes a shrubby growth and seldom develops into a real tree. It is a legume, and, although its wood has little commercial value, the tree does have the characteristic of other legumes of taking nitrogen from the air and fixing it in the soil, where it is taken up and used by many plants. The tree also bears clusters of pealike seed pods which furnish food for birds and some of the smaller furbearers. Dogwood and redbud have long been associated in Christian mythology: the Judas tree as the one beneath which Christ was betrayed and the dogwood as the one from which the Cross was made.

In late afternoon we pass the gravel roads that turn aside from our highway to Upper and Lower Hepsida schools, and then we drop steeply down to cross Pigeon Creek on a low-water bridge. This bridge is a slab of rock and concrete laid solidly on the stream bottom, with three or four large drainpipes through the base to carry the normal flow of water. When the stream rises, as Ozark streams do after every hard rain, the water comes pouring over the bridge until it reaches normal level again. A hundred yards or so from each end is a sign reading "Impassable in Wet Weather," while at the bridge itself is a white post marked off in feet to show the stage of flood.

The road climbs out of Pigeon Creek valley to top another high ridge and then, with a hairpin curve or two, goes coasting precipitously down to the Park. Although the difference in elevation between ridgetop and valley is only 300 feet, the drop comes swiftly in a distance of no more than a quarter-mile. In the Park there has been little effort at any artificial development except for the pools of the trout hatchery. There are a few acres of hilly meadow covered with a dense stand of bluegrass, through the center of which the two spring branches come pouring down. Another low-water bridge crosses these on the way to Park headquarters, and though some stone riprapping has been done along the streams to prevent cutting of the banks, they are otherwise natural and flanked by large trees. Surrounding the meadow, the timbered hills rise abruptly.

The buildings at Montauk are as modest as the other developments: a headquarters lodge with dining room, a dozen cabins, small houses for Park employees and personnel of the Conservation Commission, a service building or two. Most of these are stained brown and fit unobtrusively into the landscape, as they should. Although there is a comfortable campground, on this trip we took one of the cabins and were soon broiling a steak to the accompaniment of supper music by the wood thrushes.

I suppose that 90 per cent of the people who visit Montauk are attracted by the trout fishing; and since the stream is stocked twice each week with fish of legal size, the fishing is generally good. We do not scorn such angling and never hesitate to wet a line when we are here. Yet we belong to a school that prefers to take its chances on one wild fish in a dozen miles of stream, as

against the limit of liver-fed hatchery trout caught in a short stretch of water where one stands cheek by jowl with a hundred other anglers. Without looking down our noses at hatchery-raised fish, the matter simply has to do with what we call "trophy value" and the watering down process which always takes place when an outdoor art must be practiced under highly artificial conditions.

There are certainly two sides to this matter, and thousands of enthusiastic fishermen would have little opportunity whatever for the pursuit of game fish if it were not for the hatchery and the stocked stream. Here in the Ozarks, however, we have hundreds of miles of water stocked naturally with smallmouth and largemouth bass, walleyed pike, rock bass or goggle-eye, and several varieties of sunfish. The pursuit of these requires knowledge of place and time, habit and habitat, and a considerable skill. It can, moreover, be carried out in solitude or with the companion of one's choice.

In addition to the anglers, a few people come to Montauk merely to enjoy the beauty of this small mountain retreat; and at any time from April to November there are ample rewards for such a visit. During the spring migration of songbirds, the good observer armed with binoculars and field guide may build a list of nearly a hundred species in a weekend, even though water and shore birds (except for the heron family) are largely absent. The list of resident species is also a long one, for there are nesting habitats to attract birds of the open field, edge-cover, stream-side, and deep forest.

It is the botanist, however, who has the richest treat in store during a springtime visit to Montauk; for at this

season there is a vast variety of trees, shrubs, and wildflowers in blossom. The very age of the Ozark highland is favorable to the development of a large and
complex flora. There has been time during countless
centuries for many plant species and subspecies to
evolve and for others to invade the area and establish
and adapt themselves. Soils which form in a temperate
climate over long periods of time are hospitable to such
a complex life structure, and it has been noted that in
the wilderness state the Ozarks supported a very large
number of species of birds and animals as well as of
plants. The area is, moreover, a sort of geologic and
climatic crossroads, so that one finds here representatives of plant families from the north woods, the mountains and long-grass prairies to the east, the Great
Plains on the west, and the savannahs of the southland.

No Ice Age or period of glaciation has disturbed the
Ozark flora; and it is a recognized ecological fact that
when wilderness is not upset by such violent change, it
maintains itself in equilibrium for very long periods of
time, slowly increasing its life-carrying capacity. Thus
it is that such plant species as have become rare or
been entirely lost suffered largely at the hand of the
white man. The stripping of the forest from the hills,
fire, overgrazing, careless cultivation, and the conse-
quent erosion have been the principal enemies of the
native flora in its struggle for survival. Yet in places
such as Montauk the damage has been held to a minimum. Some of the terrain is so rugged as to discourage
logging and make farming and even grazing almost
impossible. Especially is this true of the deepest hollows
and along the streams where sheer limestone bluffs

afford natural protection for many species of plants. Such areas as the National Forests and State Parks, moreover, have now been protected against grazing, fire, and wasteful logging for a good number of years; so that even some of the rarer species are beginning to reappear.

It is seldom we visit the Montauk area in spring without discovering some blossoming flower that is new to us or at least one which does not grow in our immediate neighborhood. On this trip we were admiring the brilliance of the fire pink (*Silene virginica*) which grew in profusion along the rocky hillsides in company with several varieties of wild phlox and *Verbena canadensis*. Then we noticed another pink blossom growing closer to the ground and stopped the car to examine it. This turned out to be the beautiful pink catchfly, *Silene Wherryi*, whose eastern counterpart is *Silene pennsylvanica*. Here on the headwaters of Current River this plant crosses with the fire pink to produce a true hybrid.

The orchids have a habit of tucking themselves into out-of-the-way corners in the moist woods, but the Montauk area at this season boasts most of those that bloom this early. The list includes several lady's slippers (*Cypripedium*), early coral root (*Corallorrhiza*), twayblade (*Liparis*), showy orchis (*Orchis spectabilis*), and ladies' tresses (*Spiranthes*). The lily family is also well represented at this season by wild hyacinth, white and yellow dogtooth violets, small and large bellwort, true and false Solomon's seal, and several trilliums. There are columbines and larkspur, oxalis and wild geranium—but the entire list is too long to set down. There are, after all, 130 botanical families included among the flowering trees, shrubs, and small plants of

the Ozark highland. These are represented by approximately 750 species and an additional 1,250 subspecies. Almost without exception, some member of each family is present along the Current River watershed. Certainly the number of species would run well above 500 and the subspecies to perhaps twice that number.

Open Range

One of the objectives of our present trip was to pay a call on our friend Spencer Jones, who manages a small timber project in the hills a few miles down river from Montauk Springs. Spencer is a native of one of the prairie counties of middle Missouri who came to the hills for his health about a decade ago. He bought a tract of land with a small house on it, set up bachelor's quarters, regained his health, found that his acreage contained some good young pine, and forthwith became a forester. Like most forest-land properties in the Ozarks, this one was largely unfenced, and Spencer soon found himself host to various "cow brutes," lean sows followed by one-pig litters, and a scattering of indigent horses. Worse still, some of his neighbors thought the best way to make grass grow in the woods was to set it afire during the first dry spell each spring.

It didn't take Spencer long to discover that the trees on the few acres which were under fence and protected from grazing grew two or three times as fast as those on the outside. He fought several big forest fires, one of the earliest of which burned over 20,000 acres of timberland. Then he started on a campaign of education to try to teach the people in his corner of the Ozarks a bit of

ecology. Some progress was made, and the fire record went down—for the Missouri Conservation Commission and the U. S. Forest Service were working on a similar campaign in the area. But the overgrazing went right on; and with it the damage to young trees, soil impaction, destruction of humus, and disastrously fast run-off of rainfall which goes with these ills. In the end, Jones became a strong advocate of closing the range in all of the Ozark counties by means of a state-wide law.

We had never visited Spencer before, and we started out early on a showery morning with some fairly vague directions from the Park superintendent. The gravel road led for a mile or two down the river, then took off across the hills. We forded a couple of creeks, climbed a high ridge, and stopped once more for directions at a small but neatly kept farmhouse. The friendly woman who answered our inquiry told us we were on the right track; that, in fact, Spencer Jones was her neighbor. We need only follow the road through the woods for about a mile until we came to a white gate, open the gate and proceed until we saw his house.

We followed the road through a good stand of young pine and came out soon afterward in a clearing on top of the mountain. There stood a modest white cottage with a sweeping view in all directions. I sounded the horn loudly in case our host should be late abed, but he came out to greet us and soon had a fresh pot of coffee on the stove. When the brew was finished, we sat for an hour talking over the problems of bringing back the Ozark timber and educating the Ozark people to the fact that such a program—rather than the grazing

of a little mediocre livestock on other people's land—
will bring about the surest and most prosperous future
for this hill country.

Spencer corroborated what we have found in other
parts of the open-range country: that many Ozark people agree they would be better off with livestock under
fence instead of roaming at large. They recognize the
impossibility of controlling Bang's disease or brucil-
losis when everyone's cattle run free or of improving
the quality of their stock when rogue males roam the
woods. They know, too, that the "free grazers" are a
minority who often own little or no land, despite their
numbers of cattle and hogs. But they also know—and
it is here the difficulty lies—that through threat of fire
and fence-cutting this minority maintains the whip
hand. Thus when the township and county elections
come along with a closed-range issue on the ballot, the
majority stays home rather than run the risk of retaliation.

Tradition also affects the voters, and the legality of
open range has a long and tangled history. Many natives without a single head of livestock cherish in the
abstract their right to use unfenced land. In the same
way, they find it hard to go along with laws which
govern the taking of fish and game or laws which
penalize them for cutting an occasional truckload of
trees on land belonging to some absentee owner. Ozark
tradition has long held that land not actually fenced,
lived on, and guarded by the owner may be used as
public property. And few things are as hard to change
as tradition in a backwoods country.

5 JACKS FORK

Every river has its song, but the music of Jacks Fork is more beautiful than most. It is a tune played all day long as you float downstream in your canoe. Sometimes you hear the sparkling arpeggios of the gravel runs, sometimes, from a half-mile away, the deeper kettle-drums of the rapids. The song obscures the sound and to a degree the motion of your passage, so that you may round a bend to surprise a whitetail doe drinking un-afraid at the head of a riffle.

Yet I am not sure that this music of the river is au-dible to everyone, for it is compounded of sound and silence. It is in the harsh cry of a pileated woodpecker beating across the valley. It echoes in the evening song of the wood thrush and the plaintive little note of the pewee. It is in the graceful flight of cliff swallows at twi-light and in the silken rustle of wings as a band of teal pass swiftly overhead on their way upstream. It is in the booming call of barred owls after moonrise, in the re-iterated note of the whip-poor-will, and in the baying of hounds after a fox along the high ridges.

There is music in the very silence of the night, and perhaps it is best heard by those who have followed the trails into high country or gone out to camp in the still-ness of the desert. When the fire dies and the summer constellations start their march across the sky, you be-come conscious of the vast symphony of a universe still too large for man's comprehension.

More than most streams in the United States, Jacks

Fork has been let alone, its watershed less exploited. Its upper reaches are the closest approximation to wilderness in the Current River country. This small, swift, beautiful stream is the principal tributary to the larger river, which it joins eight miles northeast of Eminence in Shannon County.

Jacks Fork has its source in Texas County, many miles westward, where its north and south forks come together with Pine Creek to form the main stream. After a dozen twisting and tortuous miles it crosses over into Shannon at the Howell County line and thereafter continues its course along a narrow and precipitous valley. From its headwaters to the point where it flows into Current River, the smaller stream traverses a distance of perhaps sixty miles.

The chief reason why the upper Jacks Fork watershed gives at least the illusion of wilderness is that it is heavily timbered and that the valley contains almost no alluvial land suitable for cultivation. There are here few signs of human habitation, and, granted that the forest is today largely second or third growth of little value to the lumberman, it fills the valley from the ridgetops to the water's edge. Rather oddly, this valley forms a narrow strip which is bordered to the south and west by one of the fairly level, plateau-like uplands common to the Ozark highland. To the north, for the river flows in a generally easterly direction, lie the steep hills and hollows of Current River watershed.

There is another reason why this headwaters country retains its wilderness-like quality. This is that it has been penetrated by few passable roads until fairly recent years and that the stream itself must be seen by floating down it in a canoe or John-boat. But since Jacks

Fork is so small, it is possible to float only during seasons of more than normal rainfall. Even then one must catch the stream as it is dropping after a rise; for once the water is down, the task of navigating it in even a light boat is an arduous one at best. Toward the latter part of June, floating on Jacks Fork is generally at an end; while there are seasons when the headwaters cannot be negotiated at all. When the stream is high enough to run, on the other hand, nothing else in Missouri can equal it as canoe water.

Outfitting for the River

Throughout the years from 1952 to 1956, drought cut the normal rainfall in the Ozarks country by half, so that many springs dried up entirely and all the streams were at record lows. On the dry south and west slopes of the steep hollows, dead trees started showing up during the third summer; and by the fifth year the U. S. Forest Service estimated a total timber loss from drought of more than 365,000 acres in the Ozark region. Finally the balance turned, however, and in early 1957 came several months of unusually heavy precipitation. Water levels started building up again, and several times during this period when our travels took us down across Current River, we found it running high and "dingy," as the native expression has it.

Early in June, however, word came from my old canoeing companion Glenn Hill that he had made two fine runs on Jacks Fork, putting his canoe in on both occasions far up above the normal head of navigation. This was enough to whet our appetites, especially as we had just struggled through a disastrously wet spell of

haying weather when it seemed impossible to get a single load into the barns without a soaking rain on it. We decided, at any rate, that we needed a change of scene and started gathering the camp gear together for the first float trip of the season.

Each year when this great day comes, I marvel at the amount of plunder necessary to take even a two-day trek into the back country—and equally at the way in which our equipment can hide itself in odd corners where no amount of searching will uncover it. Since we will be afloat during some part of most weeks throughout the summer and late into autumn, this seems the logical place to mention the equipment which we have found necessary for floating and camping on Ozark rivers.

The first essential, unless you intend to employ a regular outfitter with guides and equipment, is a boat. Ordinarily this might be a John-boat, a craft admirably suited to downstream travel. The John-boat is built of light planking and will vary from 16 to 24 feet in length. It is narrow and flat-bottomed, with slightly canted sides and not much freeboard. Bow and stern are blunt, and the bottom at both ends tapers upward so that the boat can be swung easily in the current by a boatman operating with a single paddle from the stern. It has the advantage of light draft and easy handling; it has the disadvantage of swamping readily if gotten crosswise to the current. For our purpose, a greater disadvantage is its weight, which means it must be transported by truck or trailer and cannot be carried easily even by two people.

Our solution of the problems of weight, transportability, and seaworthiness is a canoe. For forty years a

devotee of the canvas-covered cedar canoe, I succumbed at last to a 17-foot Grumman blunt-sterned
aluminum model equipped with a little 3-horsepower
Johnson outboard. The outfit adds flexibility to our float
trips, especially when fly fishing is not their sole objective. It means we can make permanent camp on the
river and motor upstream to float back or float down to
motor back. It saves hours of paddling through the long,
uninteresting "eddies" found on the larger streams, and
it enables us on leisurely trips to fish the good water
twice or go back upstream for an interesting movie
sequence that we missed. It will get us into camp in a
hurry in times of inclement weather and, not least important, provide some relief for a long-standing case of
bursitis endured by the chief paddler.

Since weight is not all-important, we use a light, forest-green, umbrella-type canvas tent with seven-foot
floor, canvas floor cloth, and "porch," this latter being a
great comfort in wet weather. A convenient grub-box is
an orange crate equipped with rope handles; one side of
the box holds the cook kit in its canvas bag, and the
other will carry most of the food for two for a trip of
three or four days. Dacron bedrolls are light, compact,
less expensive than eiderdown, and comfortable enough
when placed atop three-quarter-length air mattresses.
We dispense with cots as being excess baggage when one
has an air mattress. A canvas duffle bag for clothes (one
that opens down the side with a zipper), a good camp
light, cooking grill, camp axe, small tarpaulin to cover
the canoe load and spread beneath the bedrolls if we
sleep under the stars (as we always do in fair weather),
a spare length of rope or two, and a small icebox—these
make up our basic load. If fishing is in prospect, there

are the rods, tackle box, minnow trap, and bucket. Finally, we take a large Ozark split-hickory basket to hold spare boots, binoculars, Ginnie's reading matter, the field guides, and my cameras. We have never weighed this load, although my guess is that it comes to something over two hundred pounds—plus, of course, the canoemen.

On this morning of our first float trip of the season we were up and off soon after daylight, having worked late the night before to stow everything away in the car and lash the canoe securely on top. While we slept, there had been rain to set the oak leaves glistening in the morning sun, and the pale green circular lichens which are a trademark of the scarlet oak stood out on the dark trunks of the trees in sharp relief. Our route lay south to Ellington, then west on a county highway which crosses Current River on a ferry at Powder Mill and proceeds on to Eminence, which has long been headquarters for the upper Current and Jacks Fork country.

At Powder Mill we found the Current running almost bank-full. The small ferry boat, which will carry perhaps two cars, is of a kind unique to the mountain country, operating from a cable swung high across the stream and using the river itself for motive power. This is accomplished by dropping the stern end slightly downstream on each trip, upon which the force of the water pushes the craft across to its mooring on the opposite side. As generally happens, our old friend Frank Sutton was operating the ferry when we crossed. Frank has a farm a few miles down the valley, and we always exchange a tall tale or two and commiserate with each other on the lot of fellows like ourselves who try to make

a fortune farming in a hill country. The tales grow even taller if there happens to be an uninitiated "city feller" aboard—running to panthers seen swimming the river or the local black bear that has been eating all the young pigs in the neighborhood. Neither of these fearsome creatures has actually been seen in Shannon County for a good two decades.

The run from Powder Mill to Eminence is a matter of only a dozen miles, but the road traverses some of the most scenic country in the entire Ozark highland. Climbing out of the river valley at a steep grade, it soon reaches an elevation which affords a magnificent view of forested ridges extending away in every direction as far as the eye can see. On this particular morning in early summer, a white cotton-wool mist rose from the river valley and a score of smaller creeks, obscuring the low land from view and setting off the high peaks in sharp relief.

After the road plunged us down into this mist and across Rocky and Shawnee Creeks, we kept a sharp eye out for deer—although there is a stretch of country along here where the people, to use an expression of British ecologist Fraser Darling, "are mad for burning." Local tradition has it that after they have burned the forest floor entirely bare each spring, they will haul in leaves and brush from miles away for the simple (and assuredly simple-minded) pleasure of seeing it burn again. Many of the motivations behind woods-burning are still obscure. The results, however, are plain enough and help make Shannon County, with its excellent potential for oak and pine, very close to the poorest in the state.

Oddly enough and in spite of these conditions, some

of the finest Ozark folk we know are natives of Shannon County. Yet a majority still cling to the old ways, and as a result the area falls far short of its possibilities for the production of lumber, wildlife, recreational facilities, crops and livestock, and a better economic and social life for its people. Nor would it be too much to say that the shortage in every category is tied up, in some degree, with woods-burning.

Eminence, a typical Ozark mountain community, is the seat of government for Shannon County, and it is one of three small towns in the entire length of Current River from its headwaters at Montauk Springs to the Arkansas line, the others being Van Buren and Doniphan, which are many miles downstream. History has it that the first settlers built originally on the banks of Current River, some ten miles away from the present location, in about 1830. But, like a number of other Ozark settlements, Eminence was burned by bushwhackers during the Civil War and later rebuilt in its present location, a quarter-mile or so from Jacks Fork. There is a story, probably apocryphal, which accounts for its not having been built on the riverbank. It seems that a local farmer or woodsman was given a contract to furnish rough-sawed lumber for the new courthouse and was hauling the boards in on his ox wagon when it broke down. Rather than delay the building until the wagon was mended, the city fathers decided to erect it on the spot. So, to this very day, Eminence lies just around the bend of the road from one of the most picturesque townsites that could be found anywhere.

Eminence knew its greatest prosperity during the heyday of the timber harvest in the early years of the century. Now it is headquarters for fishermen and rec-

reationists who come to enjoy the upper reaches of Current River. Several outfitters located here can equip parties of any size with everything needed for a comfortable float trip: fishing and commissary boats, guides who not only run the boats but make camp and cook, tents and other camp gear, and food. All the outdoorsman need bring with him are his clothes, personal bedroll, and fishing tackle. Bales Mercantile and Boating Company is the oldest of these outfitters, but there are several others who can do a good job, including our good friend Walter Martin.

Since we run our own canoe, we stop in Eminence mainly to check on the state of the river, round out our list of provisions at Bales' store, pick up odds and ends of tackle at Burl McCabe's Sports Shop, fill the small icebox, and secure a driver who will go up the river with us to our starting point and then bring the car back to town. He will also, unless we end our trip at Eminence, meet us at any time we say at some designated stopping point where a road touches the river. Unless we are in a rush, we generally stop long enough to catch up on a bit of visiting, for Eminence is a town of friendly people, many of whom we have known for three decades.

Afloat with an Irish Setter

We had decided, since the stream was flush, to put our canoe in far up at "the forks of the creek." This is a full day's run above the bridge at Buck Hollow on Highway 17, which is the normal starting point for float trips, and is some sixty miles from Eminence by river. But it is a lovely stretch of water—wild and solitary—and the

opportunity to see it comes no more than once in a dozen years or so. Just one road touches this part of Jacks Fork valley, and the chances are you will spend the entire day without seeing so much as a native fisherman along the bank.

Even with the water at high stage we knew we could hardly come down with a loaded boat, so we decided to forego camping for one night and deposited our gear at Cardinal Acres, a pleasant cottage camp located just below Buck Hollow at the juncture of the river and the highway. For the last dozen miles the gravel road from there to The Forks traverses the back country and finally reaches the stream at a little low-water bridge. Just below it is a gravel bar, and here we unloaded the canoe—along with cameras, fishing tackle, water jug, and a small icebox containing our luncheon. Once these were aboard, we bid goodbye to our driver and told him we hoped to arrive at Eminence wet but undrowned in a matter of four days more or less. After I had rigged a fly rod for Ginnie, she took her place in the bow, and I wheedled Tiger, our young Irish setter, aboard. This was Tiger's first time in a canoe. For a moment he acted as though he wanted to remain a landlubber forever, but soon he settled down between the thwarts.

There was so little water here at our starting point that I could have easily jumped across the stream. Yet it ran deep and swift, and I knew that unless we came unexpectedly to grief in some swift rapid, we should have no real difficulty. There is little reason, as a matter of fact, for getting into trouble when one runs the river as we do. Our objective is not the thrill which comes from shooting white water but rather the full enjoyment of

every mile and every sight along the way. Thus when the stream narrows, makes a right-angle turn, and goes plunging down beneath low-hanging branches into a jam of sunken logs, I never hesitate to step out in the shallow water and let the canoe down past the crucial spot by the rope attached to the stern. Once this point has been negotiated—and it is generally a matter of only a few yards—I can step in again to go shooting down the rest of the run. Although we now and then miss a bit of excitement by the use of this method, it has enabled us to float the Ozark rivers for many years without upsetting a canoe or losing any equipment.

There is an intimacy about a little river such as Jacks Fork which is missing from larger streams and accounts for much of its charm. Though you ride the center of the current, neither bank is more than a few yards away. Trees arch their branches out across the water so that you can almost always paddle in shade and thus escape the heat of the summer day. Green turtles slip from slanting logs into the water not much more than an arm's length from the canoe, and you can reach out to touch the ferns driping from the bluffs. Here are Venus maidenhair and walking fern, mosses and lichens and spleenworts, wild hydrangea, and an occasional Ozark rose growing in a rock crevice at the water's edge.

The forest growth along the banks and up the deep hollows running to the river is varied as only a midwestern forest can be. In the deeper soils grow giant sycamores and cottonwoods, with walnut and elm in the little areas of bottomland. Farther back in the hollows and starting to climb the slopes are the hickories—bitter-nut, mocker-nut, pig-nut, and the sweet-fruited shagbark. From these, in early morning, you can hear

the gray and fox squirrels barking. The varieties of oak almost defy listing; although all members of the family are present, the scarlet oak is perhaps the dominant species. A scattering of short-leaf pine is always present along the Jacks Fork watershed, this being in the heart of the Ozarks' pine range. Gnarled red cedars of great age cling to the edges of the bluffs, and the sour gum finds a foothold on rocky slopes.

Bird life along all the Ozark streams is interesting but here on Jacks Fork can be enjoyed close at hand. As midday approaches, we find a bit of deep shade on a gravel bar at the foot of a pool. We beach the canoe here to have a swim before luncheon and soon are intrigued by the distinctively marked cliff swallows which maneuver gracefully above the stream in an endless pursuit of insects and then fly unerringly into their nesting holes in the limestone cliff. Phoebes also nest in the cliff but do their hunting from the tip of some dead tree limb that reaches out above the water. Here, too, we see the least flycatcher and a scolding titmouse.

After a luncheon washed down with cold spring water and shared with Tiger, who has been watching the minnows in the shallows with intense concentration, we lie back to rest muscles tired by the morning's paddling. The beautiful melody of the wood thrush comes to us from the deep timber across the stream, and we can hear the songs of vireo, yellow-throat, indigo bunting, and the somewhat comical medley of the yellow-breasted chat. A loud "cre-e-e, cre-e-e" calls our attention to a red-shouldered hawk standing sentinel atop a dead cedar high on the bluff. A kingfisher comes rattling down the pool to dive for a minnow in the shallows. And then, far up in the blue sky, we count four

turkey vultures circling on tireless—and almost motion-less—wings. They are riding an updraft, an exercise we have long been convinced is indulged in for sheer fun. And as we watch, more vultures come to join them until there are a full dozen, all circling higher and higher. (We recall that once, peering down a deep "chimney" in the Smokies from a height of four thousand feet, we saw perhaps fifty vultures riding just such an updraft far below us. As they climbed, more big birds came in to join them, and we looked out over the valley with our binoculars and could spot them in every direction. The air currents must have been just right, for the vultures finally circled past the elevation at which we stood, and there were, by this time, fully two hundred of them.)

In early afternoon we started downstream again, pushing along a bit faster because we had no idea how far ahead our destination lay. Ginnie plied her fly rod, and though the big bass weren't striking, we were kept busy unhooking and releasing the small ones, as well as countless goggle-eye, sunfish, and black perch. Toward the end of the afternoon we began to save the best ones and soon had enough fish for supper tucked away in the icebox.

On the larger Ozark rivers which are floated fre-quently in summer and used throughout the year as a "highway" by the people who farm the narrow valleys, each bluff and pool and rapid has its name. Up here on the head of Jacks Fork the same thing may perhaps be true, but the names would be known only to the local people. Adventurers like ourselves do not pass this way often enough to learn them; although, as the afternoon wore on, we wished we had, so that we might know just

where we were. Finally, fearing we would be caught by darkness, we tilted the little Johnson motor on the stern of the canoe down into the water, started it up, and sped through each short stretch that was deep enough.

About five-thirty, we heard an unusually loud roar of rapids ahead of us and soon came into sight of the roughest bit of water of the day. This was a swift chute with a drop of perhaps five feet in a quarter-mile and dotted throughout its entire length and breadth with wicked rocks projecting above the surface and many more over which the white water broke. I stood in the stern to try to study out a passage; but in the end there was no alternative to letting the boat down by rope.

Ginnie and Tiger disembarked on the rocky shore, and down the edge I went, waist deep and clinging to the willows with one hand while holding firmly to my stern line and trying to keep my footing on the slippery boulders. At last came a "point of no return" where the rapid made a sharp bend, and there was nothing left but to climb aboard and run it. So I called to Ginnie and the setter, got them into their places, made my paddle ready, let go the willows—and away we went. But except for bouncing sharply off a boulder or two, we made the rest of the run without mishap.

Around the next bend we came into quiet water, sighted the high Buck Hollow bridge, and knew our day's journey was nearly over. Dusk was falling when we pulled into the bank at our cottage camp to unload.

As I was getting the gear ashore, two aluminum canoes rounded the bend on their way downstream. Each was obviously manned by a couple, for atop the high loads of duffle in each boat sat a pair of youngsters, fortunately with life preservers. I called to ask,

"What luck?" The answer was that they'd "put in" at Buck Hollow, a half-mile upstream through quiet water, were going to camp on the next gravel bar, and had turned over only once so far. Their destination was Bunker Hill, a day's journey downstream where we would also "take out" on the morrow. We learned later that they completed their journey in comparative safety —with two more spills but no damage to themselves.

A half-hour later we were browning our bass and goggle-eye. Twilight deepened, and the whip-poor-wills tuned up (nor did they stop until morning). We were soon abed, for the day had been strenuous, and one equally strenuous lay ahead. Yet we agreed that our first day's float of the season had been a great success.

6 CEDAR GROVE TO ROUND SPRING

Over the summer Tiger got to be a good sailor, and we took him with us to the headwaters of Current River on a bigger expedition in the fall. Two old friends came along with their canoe, and we had a guide to handle a commissary boat.

The head of navigation on Current River—and this means the highest point at which it will float a loaded canoe—is the low-water bridge leading into the tiny village of Cedar Grove. From this bridge to the head-waters at Montauk, a dozen miles or so upstream, there are stretches that will float a boat in early summer when the river is running flush. But the area is difficult of access, and the run is hard to make in a single day, so that the upper river is seldom visited by outsiders. The trout fishermen go to Montauk in spring, and there are two or three summer cottages located downstream from the State Park. Aside from these, the upper reaches of the Current are left pretty much to the mountain people.

A Way of Life

The population of Cedar Grove in the summer of 1957 consisted of four families, and one day even these may move away. The timber is gone, the land is worn out past profitable farming, and only the open range is left. When this is closed, as it inevitably will be, then nothing will be left except old age pensions and child aid; and the younger families will move to where they can

secure employment. A few oldsters whose children are grown and gone will stay to live out their lives on the mountain homesteads. Then the forest will grow again, the scars will slowly heal on the hill farms, and the little creeks—now choked beneath millions of tons of gravel—will flow once more. A way of life will have ended. Another and perhaps better way will have begun.

When we first started visiting Cedar Grove some thirty years ago, there were perhaps twenty families living in the neighborhood. The town supported two general stores, one of which served also as post office. There was a blacksmith shop that kept busy shoeing the teams that hauled logs from the woods and pointing plows for the farmers. A pre-Civil War gristmill was still in operation and boasted of its "French burrs," which are the preferred millstones for making good cornmeal. To this mill the people from along the river and back in the hollows brought their corn for grinding, generally riding in on muleback once a week with their grain in a sack slung behind the saddle.

Even after the graded road and the Model T had begun to bring what we call "the blessings of civilization" into the Ozark hills, the people along the head of Current River clung to the old ways. They depended on the forest—hacking out railroad ties with the broadaxe, cutting white oak bolts for whiskey-barrel staves, felling trees and working in the small local sawmills. Most of them, in addition, farmed a few rocky acres and ran their scrub cattle and hogs in the woods. Hunting, trapping, and the spearing of fish were part of the way of life, until there were no deer or turkeys left, the small furbearers had all but disappeared, and the game fish were scarce in the streams. No matter how poor a

farmer might be, he still managed to feed a half-dozen coon or fox hounds.

There have been few chroniclers of the Current River country. In one way this is fortunate, for the area has produced no widely read sentimental fiction such as glamorized the "Shepherd of the Hills" country in the southwest Ozarks a generation ago. It is unfortunate in another way, however, for now the record is becoming blurred. Most of the "furriners" who have invaded the region are hunters and fishermen. They float the river and camp along its banks, often finding good friends among the mountain people, but they make little attempt to record their sayings and customs.

One person who did, however, is a native of the Current River country. He is Lennis L. Broadfoot, a self-taught artist who published, in 1944, a book of portraits called *Pioneers of the Ozarks*. The drawings in the book have a primitive yet vivid and highly literal quality, and opposite each drawing Broadfoot has set down a page of conversation with his subject. Having known many of the people he pictures, I can vouch that what he reports in these conversations is both typical and authentic.

Out in one of the hollows above Montauk Spring, on a rough little hill farm, lived Misses Nancy Ann and Mary Resor and their brother Bill. Said Miss Nancy, back in 1940 as Broadfoot worked away with his charcoal crayons and drawing paper: "I reckon that people think me an' Brother Bill an' Sister Mary air funny critters, cause we don't go nowhere an' don't know nothin' —only to stay at home, cut bresh an' run the plow. But somebody has got to throw their back to the sky an' feed this ol' world."

Sister Mary's remarks are equally earthy: "We don't hire nothin' done, cause we can't find nobody that knows how to do our work like our pappy an' mammy taught us. We allers had to work in the fields 'til summer was done an' the crops laid by; then go to the spinnin' wheel an' loom an' make our clothes. Me an' Nancy an' Bill still make about all we eat an' wear, like we did in the old days. It takes backbone an' elbow grease to do it, but I reckon hard work never killed anybody."

And Bill Resor says: "When we go to build a rail fence, we allers build on the light of the moon, so the ground chunks will stay on top of the ground an' hold the fence up in good shape. If we lay our ground chunks on the dark of the moon, they sink into the ground an' rot an' the fence soon falls down. This here's my wooden nigger-head maul and wedge that I split rails with. They're made out of green hickory an' burned 'til they're seasoned an' hard."

Another of Broadfoot's subjects philosophizes thus: "I got a woman an' six kids an', by doggies, it jist keeps us all bobbin' to make a livin'! I work in the woods, catch a few rabbits and do a little of this an' that—an' my woman is a purty good hustler, too. She can plow corn, split rails, build fence an' cut sprouts, good as any man. She can shoot a squirrel out of a tree every shot. All them things go a long ways in helpin' a feller raise a bunch of kids."

There is one more of Lennis Broadfoot's folks worth telling about. This is Margaret Swiney, midwife, who lived up on Sinkin Creek and was—at the time her portrait was made—seventy-three years old and weighed ninety-two pounds. Mag says: "Aside from my housework an' the work I have done on the farm

sich as plowin' an' plantin' the crops, cuttin' bresh an'
buildin' fence, pitchin' hay, makin' molasses, nailin'
roofs on buildings, cuttin' an' haulin' cord wood, makin'
rails, drivin' fence posts an' about everything else, I
have, as midwife, waited on more than four hundred
maternity cases an' delivered that many babies to this
world, by ridin' my ol' mare an' side saddle through these
hills. I owned one mare I called Gray Doll. She wuz
a kind an' faithful animal and served me for eighteen
years. The nights never got too dark or cold fer me an'
old Gray Doll to go out every time anybody knocked
on my door fer service."

The changing way of life in this Ozark back country
that began with the graded road and the Model T was
speeded somewhat by the government programs of the
Great Depression. The Civilian Conservation Corps
gave many a mountain youngster his first taste of a
world outside his own deep hollow. These boys planted
pine seedlings and fought fires for the U. S. Forest Service in Missouri's newly created National Forests. Working with the Soil Conservation Service in its experi-
mental days, they dug farm ponds and built terraces to
check erosion and so learned the rudiments of good
land use. More than this, they developed mechanical
skills and learned how to read and write and were
trained in personal hygiene. At the same time, the older
men working for WPA built culverts and low-water
bridges across mountain creeks, constructed new school-
houses, and even erected improved outdoor sanitary
facilities to government specifications on many a back-
country farm.

During the years of the Roosevelt and Truman ad-
ministrations, power lines of the REA began to appear

along the county roads, crossing the river and reaching into the hollows. Rising livestock prices made it possible for the hill farmers to wire their houses for light, radio, and a few labor-saving appliances. High on this list was the washing machine, which generally—and to this day—sits on the front porch. Whether this is from pride or lack of space inside would be difficult to say. It is sad to report, however, that during the agricultural depression which began in 1952 and has lasted ever since, the use of these facilities has declined, even though the wires of the power company still run to the farmhouse door.

Fishing Past and Present

It was our purpose during the spring, summer, and autumn of 1957 to navigate Current River throughout its entire length in Missouri, from its headwaters to the Arkansas line. Fortunately, this junketing could be done in floats averaging about three days, so that between times we could catch up on the work of the farm. The thing we weren't able to do was float the various sections of the river in their proper order. The only difference this makes in our narration, however, is that it throws the seasons somewhat askew. Thus you may find us floating the head of the river in early autumn and then running some stretch a hundred miles downstream in late spring.

It was, in fact, early September before we managed to plan what is really the first leg of our journey down Current River; the three-day run from Cedar Grove to Round Spring. Although each stretch of river has its particular charm, there is none we like better than this

one. The stream is cold and clear from the big springs that feed it, and its small size gives it an intimacy never quite equalled on the lower river. Although it is fine canoe water, it is less easily navigated by the heavier John-boats normally used by Ozark fishermen and is less often visited by them, so that it retains more of its wilderness quality.

We planned our float down this stretch of the Current with two old canoeing companions, Glenn and Lexie Hill, with whom we have camped and roamed the Ozarks for a score of years. And since we knew the water would be at low stage, as it normally is at the end of summer, we decided to run the canoes as lightly loaded as possible. To achieve this, we contacted out-fitter Walter Martin at Eminence and arranged to have one of his top guides, Doc Burrus, join us with a com-missary boat. In this we would pack our camp gear and duffle, as well as the food, cook kit, and enough ice for the three-day journey.

The four of us left Possum Trot soon after daylight one mid-week morning with the canoes atop our cars for the fifty-mile run to Salem. Here we shopped for our food and then set off southward down Highway 19 for some twenty miles to meet Walter and Doc at the Rector Road turnoff. They were waiting for us, and with them were Earl Chilton, superintendent of Round Spring State Park, and his daughter Yvonne, who would go with us to our starting point and drive the cars back to Round Spring where our journey would end.

Although we were putting the canoes into the river at Cedar Grove, we knew that the loaded commissary boat would have trouble negotiating the shoals and rapids on this upper stretch. So our first stop was at the Akers

Ferry, some eight miles downstream. At this point the size of the river has been doubled by the 100-million-gallon-per-day flow from Welch Spring, which is second largest on the Current. At Akers we unloaded the commissary boat from Walter's truck, set it in the river, and added our bedrolls, duffle bags, and other gear to its cargo. Then we told Doc to float down to the first good gravel bar and make camp. Look for us, we told him, about six o'clock in the evening.

A half-hour later we were winding down White Oak Hollow to the low-water bridge above Cedar Grove and shortly thereafter had said goodbye to Earl and Yvonne and were pushing off downstream. Even with Tiger sitting amidship—and with our usual complement of cameras, binoculars, fishing tackle, a small icebox, and the little Johnson motor attached to the stern—the aluminum canoe floated lightly. Glenn and Lex, whose Old Town has been stripped of its canvas and coated with fiber glass, still had a slight advantage and drew less water in the rapids, for they carried about a hundred pounds less weight than we did.

The river here at the start of the journey makes the first of many horseshoe bends, and when we stopped for lunch an hour or so later, we could still glimpse one of the outlying houses of Cedar Grove. At the mouth of Big Creek, where Glenn and Lex own eighty acres on the riverbank, we found a shady gravel bar and got out the lunch baskets. Big Creek drains a long valley that runs away to the south and west for many miles and embraces several thousand acres in its steep watershed. Like many Ozark creeks, it furnishes an excellent example of what happens when the timber is stripped from the hills and too heavy a livestock load grazes the

cut-over land. Gravel chokes the stream bed until the water has almost disappeared. Even the low-lying fields of the little farms along the valley have been covered by sterile flint and chert that washes down from the higher slopes, until they are no longer productive. Each rain brings a flash flood rolling down Big Creek, while every protracted spell of dry weather shrinks its flow to a trickle. It is a story too often repeated throughout the whole Ozark highland; yet we already know from experience in the protected State and National Forests that such conditions can be corrected.

We didn't tarry long at Big Creek, for there was a good afternoon's journey ahead, and we were not sure how many times we might have to wade through shallow riffles or let the canoes down rapids that were too rough to run. As it turned out, there was enough water for our lightly loaded canoes, although the addition of the food and camp gear would have turned a pleasant and leisurely float into several hours of hard work. We had time to talk about an incredible new road being built in this headwaters country. For the hundred or more years of its existence, the outside trading point for Cedar Grove has been the county-seat town of Salem that lies some thirty miles to the northeast. Now that Cedar Grove is vanishing, a new highway is being built into it from another vanishing village some twenty miles to the southwest at a cost of $60,000 or more. What purpose the road will serve—since it will carry no traffic whatever—or what taxes from the area will maintain it are mysteries that only a highway engineer could fathom.

Although the water temperature of the upper Current is too cold to afford good habitat for smallmouth

bass, it does produce some big goggle-eye which rank high on our list of fish for the skillet. And before the afternoon was over, Glenn had put several of these on his stringer, while Ginnie managed to lure one fine, rod-bending largemouth bass into striking on a popping bug. This was the only worthwhile fish of the day for our canoe. But we were so busy negotiating the swift runs, enjoying the wildflowers along the bank and the maidenhair fern dripping from mossy bluffs, and trying to identify by song and sight the rich bird life along the valley, that we did not take our fishing too seriously.

It was almost four o'clock when we came to Welch Spring, which pours its vast volume of crystal water each day into the parent stream. Here we stopped to fill the water jugs and gather watercress for the evening salad. And Glenn and I recalled cold April evenings of long ago when we used to camp here and stand for hours in the icy water, fishing for monster rainbow trout that inhabited the river below the mouth of the spring. Trout had been planted here in considerable numbers in the early days of wildlife management in the hope they would reproduce in the cold spring water. In general, the experiment failed, although the effort was kept up for a number of years and it is possible that a few trout did raise here naturally. Aside from reproducing, however, the trout throve, and some of them grew into great cannibals that would no longer rise to a fly but could sometimes be taken on minnows. Fishing was best during the cold months of March and April, and the trout habitually fed from dusk until two or three hours after dark, then again at daybreak. Angling for them was a sport for hardy fishermen, but each year we would make an expedition or two to Welch

Spring and camp on the riverbank. For our efforts we were rewarded by some fine trophies, my own best being a rainbow that tipped the scales at 7¾ pounds.

The road into Welch Spring in those days was bad, and the last few miles sometimes took a half-day to negotiate. For several years, in order to simplify camping, we kept a tent and some camp gear stored in Doc Bolch's barn on the far side of the river. Doc came by his name honestly since, although I doubt his schooling went much beyond the A-B-C's, he had some natural talent for healing and the use of herbs and took the best care he could of the people who lived along a score of miles of river. Moreover, when we wrote him we were coming down, he would bring our gear across and set up camp for us, even having his boys cut a good supply of firewood. Also the old man loved to fish, and I've seen him stand out in that icy water in the dark with no waders until he was so stiff the boys would have to help him ashore.

Once, I recall, we wrote Doc that we were coming down and received an answer from him written with a stub of pencil on a sheet torn from a school notebook. In the letter he informed us that the road from Rector was washed out and that we'd have to come in a new way which involved letting down the rails on several fences, following a logging road along several obscure ridges, and finding a half-dozen equally obscure forks bearing to the right. "But don't worry," wrote Doc, "because where you get lost I'll have my least boy waiting for you."

It was late afternoon when we let down the first fence rails and dusk when we finally got lost and were deciding to camp on the ridge until morning. But just as we

started to unload, out of the brush popped the "least boy" and guided us to the river about a mile away. "I figgered this was where you'uns would git lost," was his only comment. The "least boy's" name was Thoris, and today he is a valued employee of the forestry division of the Missouri Conservation Commission. We see him once or twice each summer and always swap a tale or two about early days at Welch Spring.

Whenever we camped there on the riverbank, some of the native people were sure to turn up in the evening to sit around our campfire. One evening a twelve-year-old youngster told a tale which, for reasons that will appear, I will hardly forget. It was about a new preacher who had come to Cedar Grove from over in the flat country of Illinois. As a matter of course the menfolk had invited him to go along on a fox chase. They built their fire high on a ridge where they could hear the hounds as they took the fox up Razor Hollow and over the hills and down Chilly Branch to the river. The voices of the pack were ringing sweet, and the lad's father said to the preacher, "Parson, ain't that purty music?" The parson answered, "Well, brother, I can't hear no music for the barking of them durned dogs."

Just how far back this fox-hunting story goes would be hard to say. Once I heard it told by a fox hunter from the lost, pre-Revolutionary back-country of New Jersey. Then I ran across it again; this time in one of Surtee's novels of the fox-hunting Squire Jorrocks, written and published in England in the 1830's. In that version it was the bishop who had come down from London to hunt with the Handley Cross Foxhounds: he "couldn't hear the music for the barking of those dratted dogs."

By the time Glenn and I finished reminiscing, the

sun was sinking, and there were still three miles to float to the Akers Ferry and perhaps another mile before we would see the smoke of our cook's campfire and the brown canvas tents pitched on the gravel bar. So we pushed along downstream, passing the bad right-angle turn in a swift rapid where I swamped a boat one morning twenty years ago—and needed five men and a team of mules to dislodge it from the big root wad where it hung crosswise to the roaring current.

At six o'clock we sighted Doc's campfire and were altogether ready for the fried chicken that he was preparing to drop into the deep fat in his skillets. Thereafter we sat for a while, idly watching the constellations swing overhead until the moon rose, then sought the welcome warmth of our sleeping bags as the evening chill came down.

Movies and More Springs

One of the objectives of our float trips throughout spring, summer, and fall was to make a color motion picture of the river—of its springs, pools, and rapids, the trees and flowers that line its banks, the fish that swim in it, and the wild animals and birds that drink from it. Motion-picture photography of flowers is especially interesting, with results entirely different from and more satisfying than still photography. Whereas each colored still photograph must be projected from 45 to 60 seconds to impress the viewer, this same amount of time enables the motion-picture photographer to show many things. He photographs the flower in its over-all environment, shows the blossom in close-up,

and, if he wants, pictures in extreme detail its particularly interesting features.

On this September float along the upper Current, we found the most spectacular blooms to be those of the beautiful cardinal flower (*Lobelia cardinalis*). Its scarlet is set off by wild blue ageratum, or mist flower (*Eupatorium coelestinum*), and yellow black-eyed Susans (*Rudbeckia hirta*). There are also the handsome blue lobelia, turtlehead, monkeyflower of the snapdragon family, and the star bellflower (*Campanula americana*). Dayflower and tall river ironweed (*Vironia crinita*) grow on the gravel bars, and in moist crevices along the bluffs is the pale lavender obedient plant (*Physostegia virginiana*).

Autumn is the flowering season for the great family of composites. In his authoritative *Check List of the Flowering Plants of Missouri,* Bill Bauer numbers 378 species and varieties of this family for the state as a whole; and most of these are found in the Ozark highland. Among the composites blooming from August until October are more than a dozen species each of goldenrods, wild sunflowers, asters, tickseeds, eupatoriums, ironweeds, and rudbeckias. Others almost equally well represented are the mint and legume families, the latter with its vast number of trefolia, lespedezas, vetches, partridge peas, and clovers.

Rather surprisingly, there is seldom anything static about motion pictures of flowers. Almost always a breeze stirs the flower head, or an insect visits it for nectar, or a spider drops its silken web from the blossom while the sequence is in progress. We have found, in normal close-ups, that telephoto lenses operated at

minimum range give a desirable shallow depth of field, so that backgrounds have a pleasantly diffused and tapestry-like quality which sets off, rather than competes with, the detail in the flower itself. For extreme close-ups, extension tubes are used, although these require ground-glass focusing and critical exposure for best results.

There is no doubt that motion-picture photography complicates a canoe trip not planned solely for this purpose, but it also adds endless interest. We keep the camera mounted on its gunstock, ready to capture the unusual and fleeting shot of soaring osprey, giant bullfrog or turtle on a log, swimming snake or beaver. But the tripod is also close by to be used whenever possible, since hand-holding a heavy 16mm. camera even on a gunstock is an unsatisfactory business at best. No doubt some of the sequences we get could be duplicated at home under easier conditions; but it is always more interesting to get them in the field, and many of nature's aspects can be captured in no other way. A cluster of whirligig water beetles spinning madly round and round at the water's edge, a group of swallowtail butterflies drinking on a sandspit, a diving osprey— these things could hardly be set up in the studio.

In spite of the time out for photography, we make some progress down the river. Although there are no printed signs to mark them, we pass the mouths of deep-cut valleys that run far back into the hills. Razor Hollow and Fishtrap and Hieronymous Hollow—names to conjure with! One of the largest is Lewis Hollow, running away to the southwest and leading eventually to Sumac Valley. From this hollow you can reach The Sunkland, one of the huge cave-ins where the roof of

a great limestone cavern has collapsed into the depths below and the area has gradually healed over until trees grow again and there is only a small pond with some surrounding marshland to tell what happened here, many years ago.

This country on the head of Current River—and especially that lying to the south and west—is exceedingly wild and rugged. One need only study the topographic maps to realize that the cleared land amounts to less than one per cent in an area of a hundred square miles or more of forest, with a human population of one family to several square miles. Because of its inaccessibility, this was one of the last areas in the Ozarks to be logged off, and it is only within the past decade that the virgin pine and white oak have been cut for the sawmills. By the same token, however, it will take a good many years for the timber to start growing again to check erosion and run-off on the upper river. Fortunately, much of the land is owned in large blocks by forestry interests whose objective is to bring it back into production. Fire protection is adequate, some improvement of the stands is going forward, and only the closing of the range to livestock is needed to speed the process of rehabilitation.

One thing we notice about this upper river is that it is little used by even the few people who live along the valley. This is in sharp contrast to the country downstream, where the river serves as a regular roadway for the valley farmers. Here on the headwaters are almost no John-boats tied at boat landings, and such fishing as is done by the natives is done from the banks. On the lower river, each farm or access road has its landing with a boat or two chained to a tree root. The

stream is regularly used as a highway to visit the neighbors, go to church, or ferry the youngsters across to school. Gigging at night for rough fish is a favorite sport, and almost every boat is rigged at the bow for a gasoline gigging torch and at the stern for an outboard motor.

We found the whole stretch of upper river from Akers Ferry down to be even more beautiful than we recalled it from earlier years. At Cave Spring we stopped to paddle back into the cavern where the dark blue water rises in a still, deep pool almost at the river's edge. It was just above here that Glenn and I were camped one night some twenty years ago and had our worst experience at being washed out by a flood. We had chosen a high gravel bar and pitched the little tent some seven or eight feet above the level of the stream, because we could see black storm clouds that marked a heavy rain on the head of the river, even though the sky was blue above us as we cooked supper.

It clouded up after dark and began to sprinkle, so we brought the canoe up to our campsite and tied it high in a sycamore sapling. Then we loaded into it all the spare gear, covered it with a tarpaulin, and built a rock cairn at the water's edge so we might mark the stage of the river during the night. When the sprinkle turned into a steady downpour, we crawled into the tent and our sleeping bags and knew nothing more until broad daylight. When we woke, the storm had passed and the sun was shining brightly. I stuck my head out the tent door and there was the river rolling by in a brown flood just a few feet away. We struck camp, cooked a hasty breakfast, threw the rest of our gear into the canoe, and stepped aboard just as we were floated off the top of our gravel bar by the rising water.

The run we made that morning was something to re-member. The river had gone up eight feet during the night and rose eight more within an hour of sunrise. We set the canoe, to the best of our ability, in the middle of the current and tore downstream. All around us were bobbing logs and an occasional henhouse or the remains of some farmer's hay shed. When we went shooting along past a bluff, the drag of water on the limestone rock seemed to put the crest of the current a foot or more higher in the center of the river. This is a phenomenon which I have since learned actually hap-pens on swift mountain rivers that traverse the deep canyons of the Far West; and I have little reason to doubt the same condition existed on the Current that day. We fortunately met with no mishaps during our wild ride, for the chance of making it to shore if the canoe had struck a sunken log and swamped would have been small indeed. At ten o'clock that morning we beached at the foot of the highway bridge at Round Spring, having made in three hours a downstream journey that normally takes a good day and a half.

One very minor handicap to having a guide along on a canoe trip—especially on a stretch of river where you are not familiar with every mile of water—is that he chooses the campsites. In the morning, once breakfast is over and you have packed your duffle for the com-missary boat and loaded your personal gear aboard the canoe, you are ready to start the day's run. The guide then stays behind to break camp and load up, after which he starts his outboard motor and soon passes you on his way downstream. He chooses a shady spot for luncheon and then repeats the morn-ing's procedure, pushing on down to some campsite that has been agreed upon in a general sort of way.

When one canoe is floating alone—or even when two are together—it is possible to agree on the general area of the night's camp, then look over several sites until you find one that has everything. Generally this will be a small bar at the foot of a run just above a pool where the current moves along at a good rate. Here will be enough air stirring to discourage the occasional mosquito—although, in justice to Current River, it must be said that these pests are the exception rather than the rule. The pool offers an inviting place for a dip before supper and an opportunity for a bit of minnow fishing in the cool of the evening. There is a bluff across from camp and, when the gravel bar is small, a bank of trees behind it so that you are shaded from both morning and afternoon sun.

The experienced river guides who normally conduct parties of several fishermen naturally prefer the big, open gravel bars. Their sportsmen are more interested in supper than in swimming or minnow fishing in the dusk. The guides want plenty of room to pitch their tents and spread out all the gear that a large party requires. They also want a big drift handy from which they can secure an ample supply of firewood. Such disadvantages as the big gravel bar has, however, are offset by the fact that the tents are up, the gear unloaded, and supper about ready when you beach your canoe at the end of a long and strenuous day. Then there is nothing to do except mix the evening toddy and relax. Moreover, experienced guides like Walter Martin and Doc Burrus are wonderful fellows and fine outdoor companions. Some of them—and Walter is one—are even excellent cooks. Not all are like one old-timer we've floated with who always waits until the bacon fat

in the skillet starts to congeal before he breaks his eggs for frying. Then, as the eggs gradually solidify and toughen into the consistency of shoe leather, his comment is always the same: "I hope you folks likes yer eggs hard."

We were more than tickled on this trip at Doc Burrus, who generally runs a fishing boat and makes no claim to being "great shakes" as a cook. From our vegetable garden at the farm I had brought along fresh tomatoes, okra, and two or three big eggplants. Doc allowed he didn't know a thing about cooking eggplant and, what's more, didn't care for it. So Ginnie and Lexie helped peel and slice it, dip it in egg and cracker crumbs, and drop it into a hot skillet. Later on, when we insisted he try a slice and asked how he liked it, his reply was a laconic: "Well, I still don't care for it."

Days on the river always go by too swiftly, and this is doubly true when fishing is not one's only interest. On this run on the upper Current, although it was only the week after Labor Day, we began to see signs of the autumn migration. Small bands of blue-winged teal, disturbed by the commissary boat ahead of us, came flashing past on their way upstream. High overhead, a familiar "whew, whew, whew" marked the arrival of a single greater yellowlegs, forerunner of the many species of shorebirds that travel the Mississippi flyway. Bands of doves drank at the water's edge; these probably being family groups gathering for their short autumn journey to the south and southwest.

We camped the second night not far above Pulltight Spring and stopped there next morning to climb the steep path along the branch choked with watercress. The spring rises a quarter mile back from the river at

the head of a steep hollow and, like many other Ozark springs, emerges silently from beneath a limestone bluff. This does not, however, represent the full flow from Pulltight Spring; for there are two more outlets on the river itself, several hundred yards below the main spring branch. One of these comes pouring from another bluff perhaps six feet above the normal level of the river, and the second rises out of the river bed at the lower end of the bluff. All of the outlets, however, almost certainly originate from the same underground source.

In the stretch of river from Pulltight to Round Spring, we begin to see increasing signs of civilization. The country is as rugged as ever and the valley as narrow, so that there are almost no farms. Access from the highway, however, is somewhat easier, and more recreationists can reach the stream. Two or three small resorts have been developed, although these are in use chiefly during the three summer months. Yet even they are enough to break the illusion of wilderness that has held us in its grip for the past two days.

Late in the afternoon we run the last swift rapid, and the highway bridge at Round Spring comes into view. Above the bridge Walter is waiting with his truck to load the commissary boat. He drives Ginnie and Lexie across to the State Park headquarters to retrieve our cars while Glenn and Doc and I unload the camp gear and set the canoes out of the water. Soon everything is stowed away, the canoes are strapped atop the cars, and we bid goodbye to Doc and Walter. The first leg of our journey down Current River is over.

7 WILD CRITTERS

All along Current River as we floated it throughout the summer in our canoe, we found fresh sign of beaver—the stumps of big cottonwood trees so freshly cut that insects still fed on the sap oozing from them. As we pitched camp in the evening, we saw deer crossing in the shallows. And there was one occasion when we had set up our tent for the night in a little deserted field beside Mill Creek Spring and were awakened at dawn by the gobbling of a wild turkey.

True enough, the Current River country is wild by comparison with much of the increasingly urbanized United States, and one might think such small events would occur often along a stream with a watershed that is 90 per cent forested. Yet they are quite rare. The belief is commonly held that forest is the natural habitat for all forms of wildlife and that wherever we find large areas covered with trees, we will find innumerable wild creatures. There are so many limitations to this concept, however, that we would do well to examine it; nor is there a better place to do this than in the Ozark highland along Current River watershed.

To the Vanishing Point

In the Ozarks, as in many places, trees tend to grow on the poorer soils—on those that give up their mineral element slowly or from which the minerals have been leached away. Trees are more tolerant of such soils be-

cause their bodies are made up largely of cellulose, which is a form of carbohydrate and less complex in structure than the bodies of high-protein plants. Minerals, of course, are prime factors in building the bodies of all plants and creating the carbohydrates and proteins which, in turn, govern the life-carrying capacity of land. In a mature forest at any given time, however, a large part of the available minerals are locked up in the slow-growing trees. For this reason, no forest in the temperate zone—and this includes the Ozarks—has ever supported such a vast *volume* of life as was once found on the minerally rich short-grass prairies of the West where the great buffalo herds roamed.

This does not mean, of course, that the Ozark highland in its wilderness state was ever a biological desert, devoid of life. On the contrary, it supported a rich and varied fauna and flora which tended, as wilderness always does, to become more complex and numerous as the region grew older. Many environmental niches developed, and these were filled by the evolution and adaptation of countless species of living things. Food supply, conditions of cover, and the amounts of different kinds of territory may have limited the number of individuals of a given species considerably; yet the number of species was large.

Because the total of these living forms which we call the biota was almost beyond counting yet existed in a given area, it is plain that the balance must have been extremely delicate even in wilderness times. For some purposes, as mentioned earlier, the ecologist conveniently simplifies the food chain to acorn-deer-Indian. Obviously, however, the chain was more complex. The deer ate many foods besides acorns and was eaten by

creatures other than Indians. Thus it was an element in many separate food chains, as was every other life form that inhabited the forest.

If life as we observe it in untouched wilderness were not extremely stable, maintaining itself in balance without change for long periods of time, we might assume that the tangle of countless food chains on which it depends for the buildup and transfer of energy had neither rhyme nor reason. Yet this very stability which we observe to exist suggests to us a highly organized system, based upon both co-operation and competition among the numberless forms which make up this particular life community. We know that when a change takes place at any level in such a complicated structure of living forms as this, compensatory changes must occur at all the other levels. Thus if the deer in some part of the Ozark wilderness had been wiped out by epizootic disease, then wolf and panther and Indian must all make radical adjustment. Either they must find new food sources in sufficient quantity or decrease their numbers or move to new territory. Pressure on many other species would automatically increase, and adjustments would take place all along the line.

Fortunately such changes as this in untouched wilderness almost always take place slowly and affect comparatively small areas, so that adjustment is made with little shock to the biota as a whole. Primitive man fits himself into this wilderness environment, moving with the game herds and even adjusting his numbers to the natural carrying capacity of his range. The really violent change does not occur until "civilized" man appears with his axe, plow, fire, and improved weapons for hunting. The results of this arrival are always disastrous to many

creatures which occupied the wilderness environment, and there are ecologists who believe that, in the end, they may be disastrous to man himself. The reason for this is that man is also an animal; that he exists in equilibrium with other animals, green plants, and fungi; and that the violent upset of this equilibrium may threaten his very existence.

The real attack upon the wilderness along the Current River watershed began when white settlers arrived in sufficient numbers to effect a radical change in the landscape. It took only about ten years for the early settlers to wipe out the big-game species, and by 1840 the buffalo, elk, and antelope had disappeared entirely from the Ozark highland. By 1850 the black bear had become a rarity, although scattered individuals of the species survived for a few more years. The panther, an extremely wild and wary creature, lasted a little longer. Some of the big cats remained in the wildest part of the Ozark highland until the turn of the century, and a few have been reported since that time. Despite recurring rumors, however, the panther must be considered extinct in the Ozarks today.

Other species followed these to extermination, one or two more have made a decided comeback, and one or two others may have a chance for survival. The badger, passenger pigeon, whooping and sandhill cranes, trumpeter and whistling swans, ivory-billed woodpecker, and Eskimo curlew are seen no more. A very few prairie chickens and ruffed grouse survive. The anhinga, or water turkey, is occasionally seen along the lower reaches of Current River, possibly straggling in from the swamp country of southeastern Missouri.

It is easy to see how, under the primitive conditions of frontier life, an attitude grew up which has persisted in the Current River country until today. The feeling remains that there are three classes of wildlife: the useful (for food and pelts), which may be taken whenever and in any manner possible; the harmful (meaning such true predators as wolf, bobcat, and panther but also including foxes, owls, and hawks), which ought to be destroyed out of hand; and the useless (song birds, small rodents, and the like), which are disregarded unless it is convenient to kill them.

During the years from 1850 to 1900, wild game and furbearers were hunted and trapped in the Ozark country with increasing intensity, even though they no longer provided the sole means of subsistence for the mountain people. The pressure of population increased not so much in actual numbers as in relation to the carrying capacity of the land. Market hunting and hunting for sport arrived to take still further toll of wildlife, including many species which up to then had managed to hold their own. Seasons and game laws were still largely unheard of and were little regarded or enforced when they came into being. It almost seems that the attitude of the mountain people deteriorated during these years from one of utility into one of: "If it's alive, kill it."

During these years another force vastly inimical to wildlife came into being; for now the lumberman appeared along Current River watershed, and the hills and hollows were swiftly stripped of virgin pine and oak. More settlers moved in to occupy the steep cleared land and almost at once began to use fire in their effort to prevent the forest species from taking over again and to

keep the land open for grazing. The effects of this practice over a long period in causing run-off of rainfall, erosion, loss of water storage and soil fertility, and stream siltation have been set down in previous chapters. But as the land went downhill, so did its carrying capacity for livestock and for wildlife, as well. It is not too much to say that during the first quarter of the present century the 2,500 square miles of forest land comprising the Current River watershed, as well as the stream itself, were on the way to becoming a biological desert.

Probably the years from 1920 to 1935 represent a low point in the history of natural resources in the Current River country. A very large part of the timber had been stripped from the entire watershed, and much of the area was burned each year in fires set deliberately by the local people. Game species and furbearers had almost disappeared because of excessive hunting and trapping and the low carrying capacity to which the land had been reduced. The game-fish population had declined almost to the vanishing point; and here the reasons included run-off from the bare hills, which caused frequent flooding, and siltation that wiped out cover and acquatic growth. Such illegal practices as dynamiting to kill the fish and out-of-season gigging took their toll.

There were grown men living along Current River watershed during this period who had never seen a deer in the wild state. In the space of a hundred years the deer population in Missouri had declined from a total of between 750,000 and 1,000,000 to a low of less than 2,500 whitetails. A large part of this remnant, it is true, inhabited the rough hills and hollows of Shannon and Carter counties along the river. Yet even after the season

was entirely closed in 1925, it is doubtful that the annual increase in deer numbers did more than balance out the illegal kill.

The Present Situation

Unless we count furbearers, there are today just two game mammals in the Ozarks in addition to the deer, these being the gray and fox squirrels and the cottontail rabbit. The cottontail is a remarkably adaptable and persistent little creature. It is one of the so-called "buffer species" which, because of its reproductive powers and propensities for survival, furnishes food for many meat-eating birds and animals and so protects other species from being preyed upon too heavily. The rabbit is able to live in close association with man and does best in areas where there is considerable cultivated land. It survives heavy hunting pressure and predation, as well as a variety of diseases, parasites, and plagues of ticks, chiggers, and fleas. Along Current River watershed and in the Ozarks generally, poor food and cover conditions plus heavy year-round harvesting by hunters, foxes, owls, hawks, dogs, and feral house cats prevent any marked increase in population.

As for the gray and fox squirrels, one can spend a day floating down Current River in his canoe without seeing more than two or three of either species, while a morning's bag of a half dozen in season is considered unusual. Compare this with reports by Ernest Thompson Seton in 1914: of one observer who saw an estimated 100,000 gray squirrels in migration in a single day on Black River and Cane Creek to the east of the Current; and of an "army" of not less than 500,000 grays traveling westward

through Pemiscot County and reported by Sam Warren, a reliable observer of that area. Today this second most important of Missouri's game mammals is barely holding its own and perhaps not even that in the Ozark country.

The Current River watershed is a natural habitat for perhaps a dozen furbearers and as many so-called "predators." Furbearers include the opossum, skunk, raccoon, muskrat, mink, weasel, the extremely rare otter, and the red and gray foxes. One newcomer has lately been added, or at least an old-timer has returned; for the beaver is reappearing on many of the Ozark streams. Only the beaver and gray fox, of all those on our list, are more than holding their own along Current River. The beaver, extinct for fully a hundred years in the Ozarks, was finally reintroduced some seasons ago and is, with protection, making quite a remarkable comeback. The gray fox goes up and down, probably following the population cycles of various small rodents; yet it has managed to maintain its numbers fairly well for the past several decades.

The bobwhite quail and the wild turkey are the two game birds still remaining as permanent residents along the Current River watershed, although only the former is present in numbers sufficient for hunting. On a "birds per acre" basis, the quail population is low throughout the Ozarks in comparison with richer agricultural areas of the state. This is because of a general scarcity of food and cover on the overgrazed hill farms. Yet the large amount of forest escape cover keeps the survival rate high. In years of adequate rainfall or when low cattle prices cut the numbers of livestock in the woods, the Ozarks support a fair quail population. The prospects for any increase, however, are not bright. The low carrying

capacity of the land, the slow but steady shrinkage of farm acreage, and the large numbers of free-ranging cattle and hogs which wipe out both food and cover all mitigate against a larger quail population.

The wild turkey situation seemed, for a number of years, to be altogether hopeless. Predation, illegal hunting at all seasons, fire, and grazing which destroyed the habitat—all these combined to keep the turkey population at the vanishing point. Extensive and extremely expensive efforts at stocking the Ozarks with partially wild pen-raised birds met with spectacular failure for many reasons. Important among these was that the partly tame birds simply lacked the characteristics necessary for survival in the wild. Some of the birds fell easy prey to foxes and hunters; others joined up with farm turkeys and perished from poultry diseases. Today, for reasons which will appear in a later chapter, the wild turkey is making a strong comeback, and the wildlife biologists believe a day will come when this magnificent bird can again be included among our game species with at least a short open season for hunting.

Although both red and gray foxes are almost always classed by country people, as well as by many sportsmen, as predators, they actually belong in the category of furbearers where we have placed them. The gray is probably the dominant species in the forested watersheds of the Ozark rivers, although reds are found in every Missouri county. The red fox is the preferred species of those fox hunters who like to turn their hounds loose on soft summer nights and listen to them run; for where the gray will go to ground at the first opportunity, the red fox can be counted on to give the dogs a good race. Both species feed chiefly on the various families of

rodents, with mice at the top of the list. Rabbits, ground-hogs, ground squirrels, lizards and frogs, and even insects make up part of the diet. Some game and songbirds are taken, although the number of these is small. Now and then a fox develops a liking for poultry and, during the weeks when it is raising its own young, may literally clean out a chicken house. Such individuals are, however, quite rare and can generally be disposed of without much difficulty.

The bobcat (*Lynx rufus*) is universally considered as a harmful predator, although there is a feeling today on the part of most wildlife managers that "predator" is a highly misleading term. The food of the bobcat consists chiefly of rabbits, mice, wood rats, chipmunks, and gophers. It will take other small mammals when possible and doubtless accounts for a few game birds, although the number of these cannot be great. Now and then a fawn may fall victim to the bobcat, and there is no doubt that it occasionally takes an adult deer, but only if the animal is very old, sick, or wounded. The average weight of the mature bobcat is about fourteen pounds and its length some thirty inches from nose to the tip of its stubby tail, which gives an idea of the likelihood of its attacking large animals. In the Current River country the population density is no more than one cat per fifteen to twenty square miles, and no bounty is needed to keep its numbers under control.

Wolf and coyote are grouped together in lists of Missouri predators, and it was originally considered that the former was the timber or gray wolf (*Canis lupus*). Today it seems well established that the species found in the Ozarks is the red wolf (*Canis niger*). This is an animal of slighter build, although of about the same height

and length as the gray wolf, and with a tawny coat verging toward black. The incidence of the red wolf in the Current River country is perhaps one per twenty square miles; while the true coyote (*Canis latrans*) is so rare that it must be considered accidental. There is no doubt that the red wolf preys on deer—chiefly young, old, sick, or crippled animals. It will kill an occasional calf or pig and undoubtedly slays sheep. Yet much of the damage to domestic animals attributed to the wolf is actually done by dogs. There are some 150,000 free-ranging dogs in the Ozark counties as against not many more than 1,500 wolves. Granted not many dogs become sheep killers, a certain number of them do. These hunt in packs, kill numbers of sheep or pigs in a single foray, and frequently return to the same farm night after night, which wolves will not do. Since wolf and coyote are regularly hunted for bounty throughout the entire year, it seems certain no additional pressure is needed to control their numbers.

Probably the most unjustly treated of all so-called predators in the Ozark country are the hawks and owls. These are today, as they have always been, universally persecuted by farmers and hunters. This is true even though only two of the hawks, the Cooper's and the sharpshin, are true predators and on the "no closed season" list of the Conservation Commission. Theoretically all the rest, including the rare bald eagle and the osprey, are protected by the "general prohibition" clause in the Wildlife Code of Missouri.

The unprejudiced wildlife technician, as well as the informed sportsman and layman, knows that hawks and owls are generally beneficial because of the tremendous number of rodents they consume. These far outweigh

all other kinds of food in the diets of most hawks and owls, although the accipiters which we have mentioned are bird eaters. The horned owl also, it is true, lives on such species as rabbits, squirrels, ducks, and any other birds and small mammals that it can capture. In our Ozark country, hunting pressure and year-round shooting by uninformed farmers keeps the numbers of these three species well within bounds. Certainly all the others have such high economic value that they warrant complete protection.

The subject of modern-day predation in the areas frequented by our valuable game species would not be fully covered without mentioning dogs and cats. Both of these, under certain conditions, become game killers, and there are estimated to be somewhere around 700,000 cats and 350,000 dogs in the so-called "game range" of the entire state of Missouri. Of the cats, perhaps a third are strays, and most of the rest are not confined at night when they can do their most destructive hunting. The number of dogs is, of course, not as great. Yet in the Current River country almost every farm supports a number of poorly fed, free-ranging dogs that do real damage to the deer herd as well as to the ground-nesting birds and to several species of small mammals. The best solution for this problem would undoubtedly be to license cats, dispose of the surplus animals by humane means, and then encourage a lower birth rate. The dog problem might even be handled in most counties by strict enforcement of already existing regulations.

The brightest spot in the whole wildlife picture in the Ozarks is the spectacular comeback of the deer herd during the past twenty-five years. The herd has grown from

its low of about 2,500 animals to the point where deer are now found in every county in Missouri and the total population probably approaches a half-million. This remarkable growth actually began with the creation of our National Forests; a program which started in 1934 and under which a total of about 1,350,000 acres in the worst of the cut-over forest areas was acquired by the federal government. Sections of all of the counties in the Current River watershed—Dent, Shannon, Texas, Carter, and Ripley—are included in the National Forests. The U. S. Forest Service was fortunate, in the early days of its program in Missouri, to have considerable help from the Civilian Conservation Corps. This was used in building roads, lookout towers, phone lines, and fire trails, as well as in planting trees and fighting fires in the new Clark and Mark Twain Forests.

Practically all the measures undertaken in the creation of these National Forests worked to the benefit of the whitetail deer. The accumulation of land in large blocks meant the removal of many people from the poorest of the submarginal farmlands within the forest boundaries. Grazing was brought under control and limited to the actual carrying capacity of the forest range. Some idea of what this means can be gained by looking at the figures from a survey made during the early days of forest management: in an area of approximately 6,000 acres of predominantly forest land with 5 per cent of abandoned fields were found 14 deer, 378 cattle, 482 hogs, 141 goats, 42 horses, 89 dogs, and 14 cats. Under Forest Service management the goats, horses, dogs, and cats would be entirely eliminated; while hogs would be cut by 75 per cent and cat-

tle by 50 per cent or more. The deer population of the area under these conditions might be expected to rise fairly rapidly to between 200 and 300 animals.

The effective control of forest fires also worked to the benefit of the deer herd. Fire-setting within the National Forest boundaries was made a felony, and persistent fire-setters were prosecuted. Effective fire-fighting methods held the acreage burned to a minimum. Year by year the area subjected to fire on the National Forests diminished until it is today almost negligible. Even before there was enough new growth to warrant a saw-log harvest, the Forest Service undertook salvage cutting and timberstand improvement through the removal of old cull trees and useless weed species. Through this program tremendous amounts of humus were returned to the forest floor to nourish young trees which throve as the sunlight reached down to them. Also in these forest openings—no longer ravaged by fire and overgrazing—grew many plants to furnish food for deer and other forms of wildlife. These included the nutritious bluestem grass, a dozen legumes, and many shrubs on which the whitetails browse.

The program of Missouri's non-political Conservation Commission, established in 1936, paralleled that of the Forest Service. Its Forestry Division was set up primarily to foster rehabilitation of privately owned timber lands rather than to take over large acreages for the state, and thus state ownership is limited to approximately 200,000 acres. The biggest job done by this Forestry Division has been in the field of fire protection which today extends to about 9 million of the 14 million forested acres in the state. This fire protection

has, in itself, been a big factor in improving the forest habitat for deer and other forms of wildlife.

Improvement of the environment with steadily increasing amounts of food and cover has been the largest factor in the growth of the deer herd, but other things have entered in. For many years the Conservation Commission maintained wildlife refuges on its own lands and co-operated with the Forest Service in managing refuges on federal lands. Today the herd has reached the point where a large number of refuges is no longer necessary, although deer are still protected in the state parks. A program of trapping excess deer on the refuges and releasing them in other areas where food and cover conditions were on the upgrade proved highly successful, and today all parts of the possible deer range in the state are adequately stocked. Properly managed hunting seasons and protection of the herd from illegal and out-of-season hunting have been other accomplishments of the Conservation Commission.

The wildlife story in the Current River watershed parallels that in the rest of the forested Ozark country. Undoubtedly the greatest factor working to the detriment of wildlife in the area today is open-range grazing by domestic animals, which destroys the habitat for the wild creatures. In the matter of open range, it seems to me that the state and county governments, the large landowners, and the Conservation Commission are equally at fault. Certainly the idea of open range in this day and age is an anachronism: a condition under which a very small minority of the inhabitants of the forested counties maintain their right to earn a living by grazing their livestock on forest land which

belongs to other people but which cannot be fenced because of excessive cost. The practice encourages fire-setting, inhibits forest growth, causes erosion, and maintains a small number of people at submarginal levels. Yet under the present Missouri laws it will continue as long as landowners and the Conservation Commission lack the courage and initiative to end it. The landowners submit because they are afraid of being burned out; the Commission because it fears punitive action from a legislature dominated by rural lawmakers and fears also a wave of fire-setting in areas where its fire-fighting apparatus is spread exceedingly thin.

When open-range grazing ends, forest landowners will soon find that proper management of their timber lands pays a good return. And as conditions improve on the 12 million acres of privately owned forest land as they have on those acres owned by the state and federal governments, there will be a tremendous further improvement in water management and wildlife habitat throughout the Ozarks. Along such streams as Current River this must be accompanied by improved methods of agricultural land use and the removal of marginal acres from cultivation. Since all these things are certain to happen in time, the future for wildlife in the Ozarks —and along the Current River watershed—seems hopeful.

8 ROUND SPRING TO JACKS FORK

First Float

Despite the slaughter of game and fish in the Current River country, it is not impossible to find an Ozark resident who is also instinctively a naturalist. An old friend of our, the late Walter Bales of Eminence, Missouri, did as much as anyone to promote interest in the recreational possibilities of the region. Walter was an all-out sportsman who had been made a devout angler and dedicated coon hunter at an early age by his father, Senator Dave Bales of the Missouri legislature. "Uncle Dave," as he was affectionately known, published a weekly newspaper at Eminence before he went into politics, and he started fishing Current River and Jacks Fork back in the early years of this century. The country was wilder then than it is now, and logging had not yet stripped the watershed of cover. Stream conditions were more stable, and the fishing was nothing short of wonderful. In fact, Current River was considered to be one of the outstanding smallmouth-bass streams in America.

The custom in those days, unless you just wanted to sit on the bank and drop a minnow into some deep hole, was to start out by wagon over the almost nonexistent roads for the head of the river. On the wagon would be enough seasoned pine lumber to build one or two boats, depending on the number of fishermen in the party, together with a tent, some tools, fishing tackle, guns, ammunition, and a few supplies such as

flour and bacon. Once the wagon reached its destination on the riverbank, the lumber was unloaded, and the best carpenters fell to the task of boat-building while the rest set up camp. When the boats were finished, they were sunk in the river for a couple of days to swell up so they would be watertight when the party started downstream. The time spent waiting for this process to be completed was not wasted; it was used to do a little preliminary fishing and squirrel hunting.

The tackle oftenest used in casting for bass and walleye on the Ozark streams in those early days was primitive in the extreme. It consisted of an ordinary sixteen-foot cane fishing pole to which was tied ten feet of stout line. To the end of this line was attached one of those early, vicious-looking plugs about eight inches long and equipped with a dozen or so gangs of triple hooks and a propeller at each end. The plug was generally red and white and was always, regardless of make, called a Dowagiac, just as all cameras were once called Kodaks. With this outfit, which had an extreme reach of about twenty-five feet, the angler could heave the plug to the bank on either side and retrieve it slowly as the boat floated down the middle of the river. And since the sight of the monstrous lure was a novelty to the unsophisticated denizens of the stream, they charged it with a will. Doubles on a single cast were not at all uncommon, and some incredible catches were made.

It wasn't many years, of course, before regular casting rods and reels replaced this primitive tackle; and certainly these were easier to use, whether or not they caught more fish. Meanwhile, when Uncle Dave went to the state legislature, Walter Bales opened up a grocery and general store. Soon, as the fame of the

*Ozark Springs Flow from Caverns Deep in the
Limestone Cliffs*

Whitetails Are Plentiful Along the Current River

Nature's Camouflage Protects the Fawn

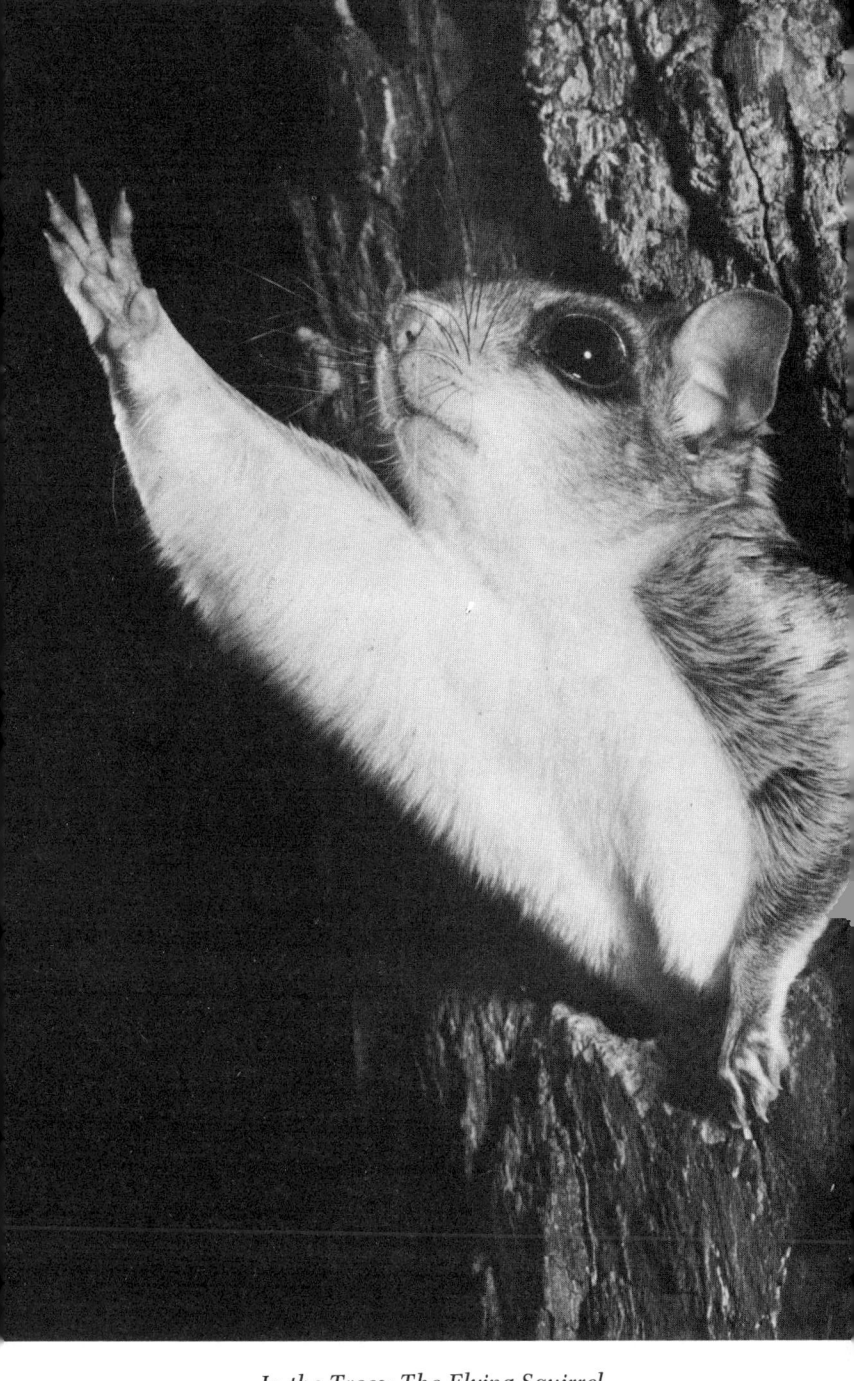

In the Trees: The Flying Squirrel . . .

And the Gray Squirrel

The Great Horned Owl, Hunter in the Midnight Woods

A Quail Calling His Name, "Bobwhite"

Red-Tailed Hawks Help Control the Mouse Population

Beavers Work Along the Streams

A Raccoon Keeps a Keen Eye on Passers-by . . .

While a Ruffled Grouse Alerts Woods Creatures

People Are an Important Element of the Ozarks

The Post Office Is a Center for Information

Gigging for Carp Is a Winter Sport

Basket Weaving Is an Old Craft

Ozark Streams Provide Serene Retreats for Modern Man

Ozark streams spread and Walter made friends with the sportsmen who came to fish them, his business expanded into the Bales Boating and Mercantile Company. He had a dozen good fishing boats built, trained a number of young rivermen as guides to run the boats, accumulated a store of tents and other camp gear, and was in the business of outfitting "float trips" for anglers from near and far.

Walter was the only successful merchant I've ever seen into whose store you could walk at eight o'clock on any Thursday morning during the bass season and say "Let's go fishing" and know you wouldn't be turned down. Unless he happened to be already out on the river, Walter would say, "Boys, fill up a grub box for Len and me for about three days. Get 'Sairy' Winterbottom and Walter Martin to run the boats. Send somebody to the house and tell Mom I'll be home Saturday. We'll start from our boat landing, and you have the truck meet us at the mouth of Mill Creek to haul the boats home." Then he would dig his rods and tackle box from under the counter, and we'd be off.

Walter Bales and I became fast friends during the years, and it was an interesting thing to watch his progress as a conservationist. In the beginning, although he could fish every day of the season if he wanted to and always caught big strings of fish, the idea of turning any of the good ones loose probably never occurred to him. His guides, moreover, were instructed to bring in the legal limits for their sportsmen by any means short of dynamiting the stream. In those days if the fisherman happened to be an amateur, his guide caught the fish for him.

Gradually things changed. Somewhere along in the

1930's Walter laid aside his bait-casting rods, with which he had developed an uncanny skill, and took up fly fishing. With this tackle he became equally proficient. But the single hook of the fly-rod lure makes it extremely easy to return a fish to the stream unharmed —and gradually Walter began to keep just a few of his best fish and to turn the rest loose. Not long after this I noticed that the guides, while still anxious for their fishermen to make a fair catch, expected them to do it under their own power. With proper persuasion, most of these fellows who are raised in the hills do not take long to grasp the idea that a fish in the stream has a value equal to or greater than one in the livebox or on the stringer.

The first float I ever made on Current River was the twenty-five mile run from Round Spring to the Junction where Jacks Fork joins the parent stream. This was some thirty years ago, when we knew very little about navigating the Ozark rivers, and Bales Boating Company outfitted the trip for us. Except that we caught few fish, most of the details of this trip have faded from memory. All, that is, except one. This was during the halcyon times of Prohibition, and on the second day our carefully hoarded stock of medicinal spirits succumbed to the hearty appetites of the guides. During the afternoon I asked Duke Martin, who was running my boat, if it might be possible to replenish our stock with some mountain dew. Duke allowed that it just might be.

That evening we made camp on a big, high gravel bar which flanked a small mountain farm, and as soon as the boats were unloaded, Duke disappeared up the

hollow. A half-hour later he came back into camp and said he was pretty sure he had things arranged. Sure enough, at dusk, as we were finishing supper, there came a hail from the timber at the edge of the gravel bar. Duke and I hurried over, and I was introduced to an old gentleman with one gallus, a flowing white beard, and a five-gallon kerosene can, the purpose of which was fairly obvious. Introductions out of the way, he came promptly to business.

"Be you the feller that wants the whiskey?" he asked. I allowed that I was.

"About how much would you want?" he queried. I said that I guessed it depended on the price.

"How about six bits a quart?" asked the old gentleman. This, I agreed, was a fair enough price, providing the whiskey was old enough.

"Well—by gravy—it ought to be. I made it last Tuesday!" he snapped, somewhat hurt by my doubts as to the age of his product.

The upshot was that, after a bit more dickering, we purchased two quarts of the "white lightning"; but I can't say we enjoyed it. In fact, if memory serves correctly, the guides inherited that moonshine almost intact at the end of the trip.

The old gentleman with the flowing beard has long since passed to his reward, and the guides who accompanied us on that float trip no longer run the river, for guiding is essentially a young man's business. Walter Bales met his death in a highway accident some years ago, and, though his wife and his daughter Shannon keep the business going, it isn't quite like the old days. Moreover, the years have brought plenty of experience

in navigating the chutes and rapids of the Ozark streams, and nowadays, oftener than not, we make our expeditions in our own canoe.

Out with the Binoculars

The run from Round Spring to the Junction is still one of our favorites. It traverses some of the most rugged terrain in the eastern Ozarks—with great high bluffs, few farms in the narrow valley, and more than the usual number of rapids and log-filled chutes. So rough are the steep hollows flanking the river that they were near the last to be logged off. In this stretch, too, are the best examples on the entire river of the great ox-bows which were cut when this area was a level plateau, some 100 million years ago. Although the general course of the stream is southeasterly, it is not unusual on this stretch to find yourself actually boxing the compass, north, south, east, west, and all the points between.

We floated this stretch of the Current in early September, making a somewhat roundabout trip from the farm to Eminence to pick up a driver for our car and then heading on up Highway 19 to the bridge at Round Spring. It was mid-afternoon when we arrived there, and we found the river slightly muddy from rains that must have struck on the headwaters earlier in the week. But since fishing was only incidental and the water seemed to be clearing, we weren't worried. The sun shone brightly in a cloudless sky, and the prospect was for fine weather.

Always when we unload the mountain of gear needed for even a short camping trip, we wonder how

it will ever stow away in the canoe, and the matter is even more of a mystery to the driver of our car unless he has been with us before. But the load is planned with care and is based on the experience of a hundred expeditions. We try to eliminate gadgets that actually add nothing to the comfort or fun of camping but to include those which do. Soon our cargo is stowed, and Ginnie steps into her place in the bow. Tiger jumps aboard into the space reserved for him just aft of Ginnie's seat. I swing the nose out into the current, grip my paddle firmly, step into the stern, wave to our driver—and we are off.

There is always a thrill about being afloat again. The canoe follows the current, slipping through the dappled shade and sunlight of the late afternoon with only an occasional stroke of the paddle. Although we aren't likely to take many fish until the stream clears tomorrow, Ginnie casts her lure into each swirl and pocket. Tiger lifts his brown muzzle to sample the air stealing down a hollow. I maintain steerageway and keep a sharp eye out for the gravel bar that will make the ideal campsite. We aren't concerned about how far we travel this afternoon, and life is reduced, at least for this golden moment, to its real essentials—a tasty bass or goggle-eye for the meal just ahead and a lodging for the night.

Our canoe at a time like this seems part and parcel of the river; almost a thing alive. It gives pleasure by its very simplicity—a supreme example of form following function. How many craftsmen, working through centuries with bark or hollow log, put their skill into the creation of this perfect form. So light that a man can lift it alone, the little boat rides the water like a

leaf. So buoyant is it that it carries without difficulty its cargo of two humans and a dog and all the worldly goods they need for a week's outing. It achieves beauty without glittering ornaments on the prow, without swept-wing tail fins, without flashing stern lights.

Boats have always achieved beauty in this unadorned way rather than by means of the carved figurehead on the bow. This is supremely true of sailing ships, from tall-masted clipper down to small sloop and catboat. It is true of the great ocean liners and even, in a utilitarian way, of cargo vessels and ships of war. So far as I know, not until recently have the makers of pleasure boats succumbed to the call of the hucksters. Now onto the working hulls of these craft are being superimposed all sorts of useless shapes adapted from the equally useless shapes dreamed up by the auto makers. Serving no purpose on automobiles but to add expense for the car buyer, they are equally expensive and equally useless for the boat buyer. But they are part of the American "fast sell" which convinces us we must buy power we don't need, speed we can't use, body designs and gadgets that are both ludicrous and a bonanza for insurance and repair man, and a chassis that is useless when we leave the superhighway.

I suppose that these gadget-infested boats belong with the man-made lakes that today dot the American landscape. Undoubtedly they furnish as much pleasure —except for the strain of paying for them—as plainer boats. They give their owners the comfortable feeling of having kept up with or gotten ahead of the Joneses. But they are out of place on wilderness streams like Current River where such useful and utilitarian craft as the canoe and John-boat still hold sway. Today the

John-boat may sport an outboard motor, and the material from which the canoe is fashioned has changed from birchbark or cedar and canvas to aluminum or fiber glass. The design, however, is fixed; it is as old as time, yet as modern as tomorrow. Moreover, the canoe is a commodity which can still be purchased for its intrinsic worth rather than for the gadgets that adorn it.

Underway on the Current, we throw these thoughts off and recall that several years have passed since we last floated this stretch of Current River from Round Spring to the Junction. None of the larger springs rise along this particular run; yet by the time the Current reaches the bridge which is our starting point, five of these big springs are already pouring into the river more than a quarter-billion gallons a day. These are Montauk at the headwaters, Welch, Cave Spring, Pulltight, and Round Spring; and their combined flow is enough for a city of 150,000 inhabitants together with all its industries and services.

As we drift through the warm sunshine of the September afternoon, however, our thoughts are far from the potential cities that may rise here in some distant future. Bird life along the forested banks of the stream seems unusually abundant, and Ginnie and I unsling our binoculars to aid in identifying the various species. Yet many of the birds are seen at close range, while others have songs or a characteristic flight pattern to make the glasses unnecessary.

Always in sight—sometimes far overhead but now and then just skimming the treetops—are from one to a half-dozen turkey vultures, those remarkable birds with binocular vision that brings them slanting down to their carrion prey from miles away and calls in their

brothers from even farther. They can always be distinguished from a great distance by their six-foot wing spread, black color, and wings uptilted at a dihedral angle. The turkey vulture is ugly as sin at close range, although other turkey vultures seem not to mind this, and is extremely ungainly when on the ground. Yet it plays a useful role as scavenger and is graceful enough in the upper air which is its element.

We find other birds of prey along Current River valley: the osprey and several kinds of hawks. Commonest among these latter are the red-shouldered and red-tailed, both of which nest here. When we see one of either species in the air, we can listen and are likely to hear the harsh "K-r-e-e-e, k-r-e-e-e" of its mate from atop some dead snag high on the mountainside. These big hawks oftenest seen along the Ozark streams are *buteos*—soaring hawks with broad wings and short, broad tails—which characteristically sweep the sky in wide ascending circles. They are called "chicken hawks" by the mountain people and are killed out of hand, which is a pity. Not one in a hundred ever raids a poultry yard, and all the *buteos* are valuable as rodent eaters. Our other native hawks are seen less often: the broad-winged, sharp-shinned, Cooper's, sparrow hawk, and marsh or harrier hawk which is another that should be protected.

The handsomest bird of prey in the Ozark country is certainly the osprey, although it would have to divide honors with the rarely seen bald eagle. The osprey is a big, eagle-like hawk that lives entirely by fishing. It is always found close to water and is recognized in flight by its white underparts, the patch of solid black at the elbow of each wing, and the very decided crook

in the wings which gives them a swept-back look in flight. Although the osprey is by no means common in the Ozarks, each stretch of river seems to have its pair. Often one or the other of the big birds will be in sight for several hours as you paddle downstream, moving a few hundred yards ahead of the canoe, perching atop a snag, and finally reaching the end of its territory, whereupon it crosses overhead on its way upstream again.

More than once as we have floated the Ozark rivers during the past quarter-century, we have known the thrill of having an osprey strike the water not far ahead of our boat, to come struggling to the surface with a fish clutched securely in its talons. Like most birds of prey, the osprey has magnificent binocular vision and can evidently see its quarry clearly from a height of several hundred feet. Its dive is made with deadly accuracy, and often the bird will disappear beneath the water in a cloud of spray from the velocity of its sheer drop. As it comes up, the fish is seen to be grasped head foremost, as though to cut down wind resistance in flight.

There are many stories of the bald eagle robbing the osprey, and we can vouch for their accuracy. On a single occasion a dozen years ago we were watching an osprey struggling for altitude with a heavy fish clutched in its talons. Suddenly at a height of perhaps two hundred feet the bird screamed and dropped its prey as a thunderbolt out of the blue swept down past it, checked on powerful pinions, and literally scooped that fish out of the air before it reached the surface of the stream. A moment later the osprey was winging up river, and a bald eagle was fighting for altitude and

soon was lined out for its nest on a distant mountain, with the fish held securely in its claws.

On the afternoon of our journey down from Round Spring we had only a momentary glimpse of the osprey which we knew had its aerie in a tall pine tree on a high ridge some miles upstream. As for the eagle, it has been missing from the Current River scene for many seasons and perhaps now visits the area only in winter. We did, however, observe many songbirds; and as we passed the deep bay at the lower end of Dugan's Chute, we started up a family of blue-winged teal. Nesting ducks of any kind are rare along our mountain streams; although we do occasionally see the teal and now and then the brilliantly colored wood duck. This latter is, of course, a dweller in the woodland and our only midwestern tree-nesting species.

Time slips away from one on the river, and now the shadows were growing long. But fortunately, some six miles down from Round Spring and just below the mouth of Grassy Creek, we found a high gravel bar that offered an ideal campsite. As one would expect after a passage of years, we noted many changes in the river. Yet the prominent landmarks came back readily. Towering bluffs, tributary creeks, small springs, rocky runs—these do not change, and we were even able to identify the larger gravel bars. Our only worry was whether we would find the one we were searching for while there was still light enough to make camp.

In this matter we have long followed the adage laid down by an old Chippewa guide with whom I camped many years ago in northern Wisconsin: that one should pick his campsite while the sun is still a full paddle-width above the horizon. In summer this is not vital,

for twilight lingers long, and the day on the river can be stretched out if necessary. Sometimes that half hour after sunset provides the best fishing of the day, although we will generally sacrifice this late fishing for the chance of a good swim and a few moments rest before making camp. Moreover, when September comes, the interval between sunset and full dark shortens perceptibly. And since we do not enjoy pitching the tent and cooking in darkness, we try to follow the old Chippewa rule for canoe camping.

The gravel bar below the mouth of Grassy Creek is a big one, perhaps a quarter-mile long and rising a dozen feet above the river. We beached at the upper end where a swift run emptied into a deep pool. Soon we found a spot where the gravel was small but not sandy and had been packed hard by the last high water. Young sycamores and willows flanked the spot where we would pitch the tent, these furnishing convenient supports for guy ropes. Nearby was a huge drift to supply firewood, and behind the camp a row of big trees would shade us from the morning sun. Across the river, that ran swift and deep in front of camp, was a steep wooded hill behind which the sun had already dropped.

When you spend a lot of time in the open, the business of making camp goes smoothly. You beach the canoe, making a line fast on shore so it won't float away as the load is lightened. Then all the gear is set out and moved in orderly fashion to the campsite a few yards away. If things have been planned here—the spot for the tent and the cooking fire—most of the equipment can be set in its proper place so that it won't have to be handled again.

Firewood is the next necessity—enough for supper and a campfire afterward and then a good supply for morning. While I gather this and get the fire going between two big logs, Ginnie lays out her food for supper and the makings of the evening toddy. Then as this goes forward, I pitch the tent, get in the bedrolls, and stow the duffle bags, cameras, and other gear that we want to keep dry. There is nothing spartan about our fare, for we enjoy camp cookery, and the amount or weight of food we carry is not a factor on these short canoe trips. In fact, the garden back home at Possum Trot provides much of the provender for our meal: creamed new potatoes, Golden Bantam corn, and a big bowl of sliced tomatoes for salad. We had hedged against the contingency of muddy water and poor fishing by slipping a sirloin steak into the icebox, and now this goes onto the broiler. But before we sit down to eat, we mix Tiger's bowl of dog food, flavoring it with suet from the steak and promising him a bone for dessert.

As we eat, a top-heavy kingfisher goes rattling down the deep pool in front of camp. This fellow spears his victims with his bill when he dives, instead of grasping them with his feet as do the birds of prey; yet his aim is just as accurate, and we've seen him actually alter his course in mid-dive, which I doubt that any other fishing bird could do. A pair of phoebes dart out over the surface of the river to take their evening meal of insects, and a wood thrush sings vespers from the deep timber.

Dusk comes as we sit back with the last cup of coffee, and by the time the dishes are washed and stacked away, darkness has fallen and a moon in the third quar-

ter is topping the trees behind camp. I spread the bed-rolls inside the tent, inflate the air mattresses, and then throw an armful of big logs on the fire so we can sit back and enjoy the sounds of the night.

A whip-poor-will tunes up tentatively, then goes into its endlessly reiterated call. A mysterious creature—seldom seen, yet often heard. I like its name, *Caprimulgus vociferous vociferous!* No less an authority than John Burroughs once counted from a single bird 1,088 consecutive "Whip-poor-Will" calls and then another 390 after an interval of a half-minute. The bird instantly flew a short distance and started again, upon which the listener went sound asleep. The whip-poor-will is a nightjar or goatsucker—the latter from an old European superstition. We have two related species: the Chuck-Will's-Widow, whose call the country people interpret as "chips, butter, and white oak"; and the night-hawk, often called bullbat. All three birds have tiny bills and weak feet ill-suited for perching. The mouth, however, is extremely large and surrounded by short bristles. These birds live almost entirely on insects which they catch in flight, so that the huge mouth and surrounding whiskers both undoubtedly serve a useful purpose.

Finally the fire burns low, and we make ready to turn in for the night. At this moment the call of a barred owl comes booming down from the hollow behind camp. This is "Old Eight Hooter," the loudest and most vociferous of all the tribe of owls and also the most curious and the one with the greatest repertory. "Eight Hooter" is accurate enough, for the call almost always comes in a cadence of eight notes: "Whoo-hoo, hoohoo . . . whoo-hoo, whoo-hooaw." When in chorus with

several other owls, however, this fellow can laugh, squall, and otherwise carry on in remarkable fashion. Give him even a fairly accurate answer, and you will soon have him and his mates perched in the trees above camp, talking away at a great rate and quite evidently interested in your campfire and other goings-on.

We stayed up long enough to hear a screech owl protest against this intrusion of his hunting range, calling mournfully in his wavering voice. And finally, from far away in the forest, came the somber, deep-voiced "oot-too-hoo, hoo-hoo" of the great horned owl, the fierce hunter of the midnight woods. We have six members of the owl family in the Ozarks: barn, screech owl, great horned, barred, short-eared, and long-eared. All are killed by most Ozark people whenever the opportunity arises; yet every one—including even the horned owl—is of tremendous benefit in the control of rodents and many noxious insects.

Once or twice during the night we woke when Tiger shifted on his tarpaulin at the tent door or drifted off into the moonlight to investigate some scent brought by the night wind; but now there was no sound except the singing of the river in front of camp. A mist came down and dripped like rain on the taut canvas; yet we knew that behind the mist a bright moon was shining. Then suddenly Tiger poked his nose into my bedroll, and I woke and knew it was morning. Without rousing Ginnie, I crawled out and shivered in the chill air, then hurriedly pulled on wool shirt and trousers, dry socks, and moccasins. Ten minutes later there was a good fire going and the water for the coffee was beginning to heat in the smoke-blackened pot. By the time my helper had rolled sleepily out, there was cold tomato

juice on the table, bacon in the skillet, toast on the broiler, and eggs ready to drop into the hot pan when the bacon came out. From the forest came the morning call of the wood pewee, the song of a summer tanager, and the cheerful note of a white-eyed vireo. Another day on Current River had begun.

White Oak and Blue Heron

Our camp below the mouth of Grassy Creek was such a pleasant spot that we lazed over breakfast and afterward took our time packing the gear and stowing it aboard the canoe. Thus it was nine o'clock or later when we were ready to resume the downstream journey. The river, which had been quite dingy when we left Round Spring yesterday, was clearing rapidly—as it always does unless the rains upstream have been torrential. The deep pool in front of our gravel bar had all but returned to its normal blue-green color, and I judged that the bass should start striking some time during the day. So when everything was packed, we rigged Ginnie's fly rod and tucked it into the bow of the canoe beside her. Then I whistled Tiger into his small compartment just aft of the bow seat, and we were afloat once more.

There is plenty of fast water on this stretch of river, and the first bit to challenge us below our campsite was Randolph Chute. This is a long, swift rapid that goes foaming for a half-mile down a rocky bank where the channel is generously strewn with boulders and sunken logs. It is also one of the finest stretches of bass water on the river. The problem in negotiating Randolph, however, lies not so much in running the Chute itself as

in getting lined out and into it in the first place. As you approach it, the river makes a sharp left turn out of a swift, deep pool and plunges into a gravel run that is narrowed to three or four feet of negotiable channel by some wicked snags which have lodged in it. At its lower end, this run piles full force into a rocky bluff beneath overhanging trees, makes another ninety-degree turn to the right, and goes tumbling down Randolph Chute proper.

Two good paddlers in an empty canoe might manage to run this rough water above the Chute if they hit it just right. With our heavy load including not only the camp gear but my movie and still cameras, the challenge was decidedly not worth the risk. But there was still the problem of how to step out, swing the canoe down through the upper rapid on its stern-rope, straighten it out at the head of the chute where the rushing water is more than waist deep, and then scramble aboard. Somehow I managed it, and then, with Ginnie holding the bow downsteam with her paddle, I climbed over the stern and we went shooting down Randolph with waves breaking over the bow. In these tight spots we always expect Tiger to become as excited as we are, but he never does. His faith in us seems complete—plus which, although I doubt he thinks about this, he can swim like an otter in any kind of water.

Randolph Chute and the long pool below it are named for the Ozark family which has lived here since Current River valley was settled back in 1836. The Randolph farm lies in a big bend in the river and is a good one, as mountain farms go. Its proprietor for many years was Will Randolph, who was not only a farmer but also the

neighborhood blacksmith, carpenter, cabinetmaker, and all-round artisan. He lived in a frame house of considerable size, set on the "second bench" above the bend in the river and safely out of reach of high water. Not far from the house and log barns was the blacksmith shop which, even after the old man was well along in his eighties and had retired, was still an interesting place. Inside and outside the shop could be found all the oddments of four generations of primitive mountain living: wheel hubs and the wide iron tires of log wagons, an ox yoke or two, a bull-tongued plow, wheat cradles, and the rest.

Even after Will Randolph had stopped blacksmithing, his neighbors still came to use the shop and the tools—many of them hand-fashioned—that hung above the carpenter benches and the anvil and forge. A hundred yards or so away from the shop, standing on a knoll, was a huge white-oak tree. This had been used, in pre-Civil War days, as a "fur press." At that time a storekeeper and trader named Deatheridge lived nearby (the name is still a common one in the neighborhood), and he took most of his currency in the form of pelts and furs. Once every so often these were baled up for transportation to the distant city. A deep notch had been chopped into the trunk of the oak tree near the ground, and in this was thrust the butt end of a long pole. Under this pole the folded skins were piled, and then weight was applied to the free end. Thus the skins were compressed tightly and could be bound into bales for shipment.

Old man Randolph is long gone, and it has been some years since we have pulled in at the rough landing on the east side of the river and climbed the hill

to the farmhouse. Across the river from the farm, however, lies a forested area that contained, until very recently, some of the largest virgin white-oak trees in the country. This tract was part of a large acreage originally owned by a cooperage company which manufactured white-oak barrel staves, chiefly for the ageing of Bourbon whiskey. In the steep hollows running down to the river and in the deeper alluvial soils found in the valley, the white oaks grew to giant size. But the terrain was so rough that the area had not been logged.

During World War II the holdings of the cooperage company, which totaled some 80,000 acres and constituted probably the largest stand of virgin white oak remaining in America, were purchased by one of the distillery combines. The distillers set up the area as a "perpetual tree farm," advertised widely what splendid conservationists they were, and employed a topnotch forester to supervise the harvest of the big oaks on a sustained-yield basis. What this actually meant was cutting the individual trees as they passed maturity and began to deteriorate. But one day the distillers decided to fill a need for cash by liquidating some of their assets rather than going into the public market for money. In a little more than two years they cut every white oak large enough for barrel staves on the entire 80,000 acre tract.

This story seems an example of the all too frequent attitude of American industry toward natural resources; yet the outcome in this case was not a total disaster. The stand of white oak was mature, which means that many of the trees had reached an age of 200 years or more. But a white oak must be at least 14 inches at breast height to make a stave tree; and even after these

were harvested, there were a great many trees left. Some of these were smaller white oaks, but there were also extensive stands of pine seedlings, some pine of larger size, and other species of hardwoods such as scarlet and black oak, hickory, and sour gum. A large part of the acreage was eventually acquired by a young businessman, Leo Drey of St. Louis, who has accumulated something like 130,000 acres of timber land in a long-range forestry project and is today perhaps the largest individual landowner in the Ozark highland.

Through an agreement made with the distillery people at the time they were harvesting the big oaks, a small area was left uncut on the bank of Current River at Randolph Hole. Here are some of the largest white oaks as well as splendid specimens of the other oaks, hickory, and gum; and these will be preserved so that future generations may know what our forests looked like before they were despoiled by the lumberman.

As our canoe drifted along close to the bank opposite the stand of big trees, I noticed a mud slide coming down into the river and paddled to shore to see what had made it. We climbed the bank and the first thing we found was a huge freshly cut cottonwood tree, the work of a family of beavers. Sap still oozed from the trunk, and many insects fed on it. The task of cutting the smaller branches from the tree had just started, and these were evidently being pulled into the river, then floated downstream and across to bank dens on the far side.

It has been almost twenty-five years since the first planting of a family of beavers was made on the headwaters of Current River, some forty miles above the

place where we found this colony. For a long time it was difficult to tell whether they had established themselves or not, for beavers are notable travelers and move long distances during the warm months. But finally, after an absence of more than a hundred years, there is no mistaking that the beaver has returned to the Ozarks. Today we find these interesting engineers of the animal world well-established along the entire Current River watershed and on most other Ozark streams.

Unlike beavers that live in areas with sluggish streams which can be easily dammed, most of our beavers are bank dwellers. Here and there along the Current in backwaters and eddies that we call "bays," one may find the beginnings of a dam. But the sudden, violent floods that roll down our Ozark rivers make dam building an unprofitable occupation and, in any case, I doubt that big dams which create extensive ponds are necessary for the beavers in our latitude. It seems probable that in a cold climate where the ice freezes a foot or more thick, beavers must have a pond a dozen feet or so in depth in which to store their supply of willow, cottonwood, or other species that provide the succulent bark for their winter food. Here in the Ozarks with mild winter temperatures and swift-running spring-fed streams, ice is not a factor, and the animals can come and go from their bank burrows all winter long. They will, it is true, cut and store a supply of limbs; yet they will hardly ever experience more than a day or two at a time when the water is not open.

Throughout Missouri as a whole the beaver has already increased to the point where a trapping season has been opened. The fur business with the exception of

mink, however, is in such a bad state that few beavers are taken. Wildlife biologists have lately developed a theory that normal cyclic variations in furbearer populations can be avoided and a high plateau of abundance maintained year after year simply by taking what they call a "maximum sustained harvest" each year.

As far as we know, the beaver population is not cyclic. My feeling about the other furbearers is that cyclic variations in population have many causes and may occur regardless of the harvest and that numbers depend in final analysis on the carrying capacity of the habitat for the species. In the case of the beaver, there is certainly plenty of room along our hundreds of miles of streams. The food supply is at least fair, and carrying capacity may depend chiefly on stream stability which, in turn, depends on the condition of the watershed. Since the state of the Ozark watersheds is gradually improving, the number of beavers can be expected to increase for some time to come.

Not far below the Randolph place we encountered another stretch of rough water—this one a long, swift chute filled with a tangle of sunken logs—which several of the river guides had told us they managed to negotiate in their John-boats with powerful outboard motors. Here there was no chance of wading to let the canoe down by rope; but fortunately the river split into two channels around an island. The smaller channel shoaled out in several places until we had to walk and drag the boat over the shallows, but at least we didn't swamp it.

Below this rapid the river makes two great oxbows, once again boxing the compass completely. Around one of the oxbows is a stretch of fast and rocky water that has always seemed to us one of the most beautiful on

Current River. The left bank is low with sycamores and willows growing to the water's edge, and on the right the forested mountain climbs steeply to a height of several hundred feet. In times of low water this is not an easy stretch to run, for countless boulders lie just beneath the surface. On this day, however, the stream was flush, and we needed only to watch out for a few big rocks. I held the canoe back as much as possible, Ginnie dropped her fly over against the bank, and it wasn't long until our supper was on the stringer—a fine pair of twelve-inch smallmouth.

Once more, as the day slipped by, we found the bird life interesting. Just opposite the shady spot where we stopped for luncheon was a clay bank perhaps twenty feet high, and we saw that this was full of small holes. We watched these with our binoculars and soon discovered not only a colony of bank swallows but also the nesting holes of two pairs of kingfishers. The bank swallows are somewhat drab in comparison with the brightly colored barn and cliff swallows. Yet they are graceful on the wing, and we would sometimes see them fly directly into the tiny openings of their nests. If they checked speed at all as they came in, it was impossible to tell it.

Bank swallows and kingfishers are almost the only American birds that nest in holes in the ground which they themselves excavate, and so it is not unnatural to find them together. The kingfisher is, of course, twice as large as the barn swallow and is a bird of entirely different habit. Yet the two get along amicably and are often found nesting side by side in the same clay or sand bank. In the environs of civilization where angling is an artificial sport depending on "planted" fish, the

kingfisher is likely to be persecuted as a potential enemy of the game species. The truth is that he lives on minnows and other shallow-water fish that are pests to the angler. He also, however, includes in his diet crayfish, frogs, and many noxious insects which he takes when the fishing is poor. He is, moreover, an individualist and as interesting to watch as any bird along the stream. From our observation, each pair or family of kingfishers has its own hunting territory from which any intruder is promptly driven away.

When you think of the tremendous skill exercised by the kingfisher in his angling, it is impossible not to have considerable respect for this cheerful and aggressive fellow with his bright blue coat, belt and crest, white collar, oversized head, and huge bill. Incidentally, this is one American bird in which the female has more decorative coloring than the male, for Mrs. Kingfisher sports a sort of reddish waistcoat. I think not even the eagle has keener eyesight than the kingfisher, which can drop unerringly from a perch fifty feet above the water and come up with a wriggling minnow clutched securely in its bill.

There is a legend about the kingfisher, which is called the Halcyon in Europe, that is worth recounting. It seems that Alcyone, the daughter of Aeolus, grieving for her husband who had been shipwrecked, threw herself into the sea, where she was changed by the gods into a kingfisher, called Halcyon by the Latins. Pliny says: "The Halcyons lay their eggs and sit about mid-winter when the daies be short; and the time whiles they are broodie is called the halcyon daies; for during that season the sea is calm and navigable." The belief was that the seven days preceding the winter solstice were used

for building the nest and the days immediately following for laying and hatching the eggs. These were called the "halcyon days," and even now in the Mediterranean countries they are a time of picnics and outings along the sea beaches, on quiet streams, or in the woods and fields.

Many representatives of the heron family are found along the Ozark rivers in summer, and most of these we will glimpse in a float of two or three days. Probably the one oftenest seen is the eastern green heron, which goes by the less dignified names of Fly-up-the-creek or shitepoke. This rather small heron with short legs seems clumsy and befuddled when you put him to flight and he goes flapping up to make a precarious landing on a willow branch. Yet the impression is soon changed if you watch this fellow at his fishing; for he has an eagle eye and is expert at the art of spearing minnows, frogs, salamanders, and similar food with his long, sharp bill.

The eastern green heron generally appears blue or black from a distance but, close up, is quite distinctively marked with blue-green back and crest and brown underparts. The bird has the interesting habit of "freezing" when flushed from the water to a perch in the willows, probably in an effort to escape observation. Of all the herons, I believe that only the eastern green and the bitterns build solitary nests; the rest preferring to gather in colonies during the breeding season.

The great blue heron, which stands four feet tall and has a six foot wing spread, is certainly the most spectacular of our herons. We have never discovered the nest of the great blue on Current River; yet we are quite sure he hatches his young here, since we often see the big birds in family groups in late summer. Earlier

in the summer, each pair seems to claim a territory, very much like the osprey which we have already described. As we float downstream, one of the great blue herons will often precede us, flapping ahead of the canoe for an hour or more. When he reaches the end of his "beat," however, we will always see him crossing overhead on his return journey.

The little blue heron is not normally a denizen of the Ozark streams. Yet the young of this species, which keep the white plumage of infancy until they are two years old, have the odd habit of wandering far afield in late summer and autumn. Often we see whole families of them along Current River, and only occasionally are they accompanied by the adult birds. If one were not familiar with their coloration, he might easily mistake the young little blue herons for either the American or snowy egret. Neither of these latter nests along the Ozark rivers; yet both appear here in autumn, perhaps having traveled all the way from the Gulf. Distinguishing the birds is not difficult if one remembers that the American egret is quite large with yellow bill and dark legs and feet; the snowy is small with black bill and legs and bright yellow feet; and the immature little blue heron is of medium size with dark bill, legs, and feet and very often a slightly bluish cast to at least a few of its feathers.

Three other herons are seen occasionally along the Current, these being the American and least bitterns and the black-crowned night heron. I consider it doubtful that any of them nests along the stream. There is, however, one more large wading bird that we sometimes see in autumn. This is the immature wood ibis, which, like some of the herons, is a great traveler after

the breeding season is over and the young are on the wing. The wood ibis is our only true stork. He stands four feet tall, has a wing spread of nearly six feet, is white with black wing patches, and has an odd bald head. Unlike the herons, he flies with neck outstretched and alternately flaps and sails. Sadly, this interesting bird which was once plentiful in Florida and along the Gulf Coast is today threatened with extinction because of the destruction of nesting rookeries through drainage and heavy logging of the last stands of cypress in the South.

On this second day of our journey from Round Spring to the Junction, we pulled in rather late to camp on a tiny gravel bar above the mouth of Brushy Creek. Here a towering bluff across from us shut off the setting sun so that twilight came early. We went for a swim which, in the 75-degree water, was refreshing; but we didn't linger long, because the heat of the September day had died with the coming of dusk.

Thereafter we doubly enjoyed the evening toddy while the bass browned in the skillet and I pitched the tent and got in the duffle bags and other gear. After supper the moon came up over the trees down river to compete with the light of our campfire. But it had been a fairly strenuous day, and not long after we had finished the second cup of coffee, washed the dishes, and made everything ready for the night, we were glad to seek the comfort of our bedrolls. For once, Tiger was as tired as we were and slept the whole night through.

9 JACKS FORK TO VAN BUREN

Names To Conjure With

Once or twice during a Missouri summer there comes a perfect week for a float trip. Float trips, however, must be planned ahead, and so one takes a chance on the skies overhead, the condition of the stream, and the way the fish are striking. In July we went on a long-planned jaunt with Ed and Adelaide Cherbonnier of St. Louis—two outdoor companions of many years—and ran the beautiful three-day stretch of Current River from the mouth of Jacks Fork to Van Buren. Water, weather, the finny warriors, and good comradeship all conspired to give us one of the most enjoyable expeditions we have made in many a day.

When you know a stream as intimately as we do the Current, it becomes quite impossible to say that one part of it is a favorite over any other. The best compromise is to agree that whatever stretch we happen to be floating at a given moment is the one we like best. This particular run, which covers a downstream distance of about thirty-six miles, boasts two of the large and interesting springs—Blue and Gravel. These plus the tributary Jacks Fork add enough water to the flow so that navigation becomes a bit easier than it is farther upstream. Yet the river runs swift as always, the scenery is picturesque, and there is always a good campsite around the next bend.

We had agreed that the Cherbonniers would stop at Possum Trot for late luncheon on the way to Emi-

nence, where we would spend the night in order to get an early start down river next morning. Before they arrived at the farm, I had finished packing our car, with the canoe on top, ready for a fast takeoff. Thus we left at three o'clock with an easy trip ahead that brought us to our destination at six. The afternoon was slightly overcast, yet there was no feeling of rain in the air, and we were grateful for a cessation of the heat that had held the Ozarks in its grip for the past two weeks.

Although Ginnie and I were taking our canoe and small outboard motor as usual—and eight-year-old grandson Ricky for supercargo—Ed and Adelaide had made arrangements for fishing and commissary boats and guides. These latter would be our old friend Walter Martin and his brother Tom. Walter operates the Martin Boating Company out of Eminence, outfitting float trips on the Current, Jacks Fork, and Eleven Point Rivers, and the two brothers represent a breed of rivermen that is, sad to say, rapidly dying out. They know the streams as one knows the palm of his hand, and both are good workers who understand what is needed in the way of boats and equipment for a successful river trip. Among other qualities, Walter is an unusually good outdoor cook. Tom has a little farm on the river, works as a carpenter in town, and guides now and then because he likes it. Both he and Walter got their first training with Bales Boating Company, the first of the Current River outfitters, and then worked with our good friend Garland Winterbottom, whose business Walter Martin more or less inherited after Garland died several years ago.

During the years we have known a very large majority of the guides who have run boats on the Ozark

streams. No matter how unlike they may be as individuals, they have certain qualities and characteristics in common. They are, to a man, natural-born sportsmen and superlative woodsmen. They are steady and unexcitable, with good judgment in the pinches. They are hard workers and willing. Otherwise, why choose a career that demands long hours of hard work under conditions that are pleasant only if your fishermen happen also to be good sportsmen? As to temperament, we've known guides who joked and sang all day long; others who were rather shy and retiring; but none who couldn't take things as they came. By and large, they tend toward being lean and wiry. Yet some are tall and some small, some even fairly fat, which is surprising. One and all, they are good fellows whose companionship we enjoy.

The little village of Eminence, which is our starting point for this trip, is in the heart of a great recreation area and has ample accommodations for fishermen and vacationists; yet is a long way from being a luxury resort town. In fact, more than any village we know, it retains the flavor of the Ozark backwoods community. We had engaged rooms at the Riverside Hotel, a small main-street hostelry that is always neat and clean, even though its "facilities" are located at the far end of the hall. After a good supper, we repaired to a bench on the sidewalk in front of the hotel where we could visit with old acquaintances and watch the life of the community flow by. Tom and Walter Martin came along in Walter's pickup truck, and we made our final arrangements for morning. We walked around the corner to McCabe's Sporting Goods Store for a few odds and ends of tackle. The radio brought the ball game, and we could hear the wave of comment all down the street when

the Cardinals scored a run. Even after we'd gone to bed, the sounds of the village street drifted up to us, but without the frenzied quality that city noises have. After things quieted down at about nine-thirty, a whip-poor-will tuned up almost outside the window, and a hound barked "treed" at the edge of town not far away.

Next morning we are up bright and early, and, as soon as breakfast is over, we pack for the fifteen-mile drive to the Junction where Jacks Fork joins the Current and which is the starting point for our float. Tom and Walter have already taken off with the truck, which is loaded with two boats, the icebox, tents, food, and other gear. We pick up two drivers for our cars, who will bring them back to Eminence and then meet us in Van Buren at the end of our trip three days from now. At the river we find the boys sliding the two John-boats from the truck into the water. One of these boats, guided by Tom, will carry Ed and Adelaide with their fishing tackle and personal gear, as well as a small ice-box, water jug, and minnow trap and bucket in case Ed wants to stop for a bit of live-bait fishing in some likely hole. Into the other boat—the "commissary"—is being loaded the mountain of camp gear, food, and other equipment that six people need for a comfortable three-day outing. This commissary boat, although built like the fishing boats, is somewhat larger in order to carry its huge load. Both it and the fishing boat are equipped with outboard motors, a thing unheard of in the old days. In the case of the commissary especially, however, the motor takes a lot of the punishment out of navigating the heavy craft.

We add our bedrolls, duffle bags, and other heavy equipment to Walter's load. Then we lift the light alu-

minum canoe from atop the car and set it in the river, thereafter loading aboard our tackle and the cameras, binoculars, and such small gear as we want close at hand. Once everything is ready, we all help Walter push off, and he winds up his motor and starts downstream, telling us he will beach in the shade opposite the mouth of Blair Creek for the noon hour and have lunch ready when we get there. Next go Ed and Adelaide, with Tom swinging an easy paddle and soon disappearing around the bend. Finally, when I have rigged Ginnie's fly rod with a gold spinner and a small brown streamer fly dressed with a bit of split pork rind, we are ready to follow them. Ginnie steps into the bow, Rick takes his place amidships, I push the canoe into the current—and we are afloat once more on this most beautiful of Ozark streams. The morning is delightfully cool, with just enough overcast to make us hope for good fishing. A little green heron salutes us with his harsh call as we round the bend, and we can feel in our bones that a good journey is in prospect.

Several times as we glide along those first miles, we hear a hound pack baying along the high timbered ridges above us. When we catch up with Tom's boat after an hour or so, he tells us a doe has just crossed in the shallows below them. This illegal running of deer with dogs regardless of season is all too common throughout the whole Ozark highland and is not an easy thing to stop. The game-law violators in a given community are generally a small clique whose identity is fairly well known, but this does not mean it is easy to apprehend them. A good many of the back-country people, in the old poacher's tradition, tend to sympathize with the violators. Others hesitate to turn informer be-

cause they fear retaliation—haystacks burned or fences cut.

The enforcement agent is almost always a hard worker and a sincere officer of the law. But he can only cover so much ground and has many other tasks to attend in addition to chasing illegal deer hunters. In the smaller county-seat towns of the Ozarks it is easy enough to know when the agent leaves on his rounds in the morning and in what direction he is traveling. Once this is ascertained, the deer hunters load their hounds into a pickup truck and make for the opposite side of the county. A good deal of this illegal hunting goes on in close proximity to the river, since a deer heads for water at some known crossing when hard pressed by the hounds and can often be killed there with little difficulty.

One wonders what happens to the venison from deer thus killed, and the answer lies in the home freezing unit which can be found today on many a backwoods farm that is served by an REA power line. No longer need the meat spoil and be lost. There are, in addition, always a few unscrupulous restaurant and club owners in the larger towns and cities who find it smart to serve illegal venison and who will pay a good price for a fresh deer carcass regardless of season. For many years prosecution in the backwoods counties where most of the deer-law violations took place was extremely lax, and convictions were rare. This situation is changing, however, and it seems possible that, with vigorous prosecution and stiffer penalties, illegal deer hunting may go into a decline. As the climate of opinion changes, moreover, there is less sympathy for violators,

and more information trickles in to the enforcement agent and the county prosecutor.

The place names along Current River are something to conjure with. Every bluff and pool and rapid has its proper designation, and when you spend considerable time on the stream, these names became as familiar as the streets of your home neighborhood. Even when you have been away for a season or two, it is surprising how soon they come back. Not far below the Junction is Coot Chute, a swift and rocky run that curves around the base of Coot Mountain. This high knob boasts a fire tower atop its summit and rises to an elevation of 1,300 feet, some 600 feet above the surface of the river. We float swiftly down through this bit of fine fishing water, and Ginnie casts to the rocky bank; nor are we surprised when she connects with a pair of good goggle-eye and a smallmouth bass of fair size that puts up a battle in the fast current. All of these we place on our stringer to transfer to the live box in Tom's boat as a start toward tomorrow night's supper.

Next familiar spot as we drift along is Red Rock, and then we round a bend and pitch into the swift gravel run that empties into Goose Bay. This dark pool swirls at the base of huge red granite boulders and in years past has produced some monstrous walleyed pike, which we call "jack salmon" in the Ozark country. There's a high gravel bar opposite the red boulders and the bluff that rises behind them, and in the early days we used to like to camp here. The big "jacks" fed at night or just before dawn and could sometimes be lured into striking on a six-inch chub minnow fished with a heavy sinker and far down in the current.

A half-mile below Goose Bay we come to the shady gravel bar opposite the mouth of Blair Creek, which drains some of the roughest country on the entire watershed of Current River. Here we find Walter's commissary boat pulled up on the beach and a table spread in the shade for luncheon. And just in case you wonder how a good Ozark guide treats his fishermen, let me list Walter's menu. Since the day is warm, he has planned a cold meal. In the center of the table is a white granite bowl filled with salad—quartered head lettuce, sliced tomatoes, and sweet Bermuda onions—with bottles of French dressing and mayonnaise on the side. A ten-quart coffeepot holds two gallons of iced tea, with sugar and lemon to taste. There are a platter of ham, a bowl of crisp potato chips, a jar of peanut butter, another of pickles, and still another of jam, along with a fresh loaf of bread, crackers, and butter from the icebox. Chilled peach halves round out the repast.

There is time for a refreshing dip in the river before we sit down to eat, and afterward it is not surprising that Ed and the girls spread out their bedrolls in the deepest shade for a nap. Walter and Tom make short work of the camp chores, and while they clean up, Ricky and I paddle to the head of the pool to try with live minnows for a bass. By two o'clock we have added a nice pair of smallmouths to our catch, and Walter is ready to start downstream again in the commissary boat. We agree on a campsite for the night just above Buttin Rock, some eight miles farther along; and a half-hour later we follow after Walter in the canoe, leaving Adelaide and Ed still dozing.

The farms along this stretch of the Current are more numerous than they are farther upstream. Yet they are

still small, tucked into the mouths of hollows that run down to the river or into narrow strips of alluvial land in the valley itself. Seldom are these visible as one floats along in his boat. We are chiefly conscious of the timber and the giant bluffs that rise a sheer 300 feet out of the water and then climb another 200 to the top of some forested ridge. Trees run to the water's edge, and the only sign of human habitation is the occasional landing with its John-boat tied to a tree root. Once in awhile we hear the distant sound of a valley farmer urging his mules along as he plows some gravelly field.

We drop on down past the old Williams Ford, no longer used, and the mouth of Bloom Creek, which comes in as a trickle over a high clay bank. Then follows the long, rocky bluff on the right that marks Owl's Bend, and we see the cable of Powder Mill Ferry where we crossed by car late yesterday on the way to Eminence. Frank Sutton, the ferryman, dozes in the shade, and we give him a shout and a wave. Soon afterward we drop down over Booming Shoal, a bit of swift water with a delightful name that sweeps beneath an old leaning birch tree and then straightens out to end where Blue Spring pours its vast volume of crystal-clear water into the river.

This whole stretch of the Current seems especially rich in bird life, and we feel sorry for fishermen who float along without ever seeing or hearing these denizens of the stream banks and the woodland. This is one thing we enjoy about camping with the Cherbonniers, who are good ornithologists. There aren't many fly fishermen who can tell you when you stop for luncheon that they have spotted the prothonotary warbler and the Louisiana water thrush during the morning's run.

Nor are there many who can identify the oven bird by its song, that plainly says "teacher, teacher, teacher" and always comes from the depths of the forest, or the white-eyed vireo, whose note is best translated "chip-oh-wee-ooo." Comparing records during the lunch hour, we found that we had all seen the great blue heron, green heron, least bittern, American egret, and little blue heron among the wading birds that frequent the stream. Once as we paddled up a small backwater bay to try for a largemouth bass in the lily pads, Ricky spotted a male wood duck; but it was Ed who saw and identified the immature wood ibis, our rarest bird for the trip.

There was one more incident with the birds that occurred on this day's trip and is worth recounting. Ginnie wore her favorite fishing hat, a vivid red featherweight felt sold by L. L. Bean at Freeport, Maine. Several times during the afternoon we had seen hummingbirds darting across the river, and one of these finally must have decided Ginnie's hat was a giant hibiscus flower. For several minutes it circled the hat as if to light, and we worried for a time that it might strike Ginnie's eye with its needle-sharp bill. At last I cranked up the outboard, and the determined hummingbird took its departure.

At Blue Spring we beach the boats to visit with our friends Hugh and Eileen Denny, at that time proprietors of Blue Spring Lodge. Then Rick starts a badminton game with their two youngsters whom he knows from other visits, while the rest of us hike the quarter-mile along the rushing spring branch to where the water rises silently from beneath the encircling bluff. At this time in late summer, Blue Spring is at its clearest. The

water now is an intense blue, an effect created by the purity of the fifty-foot water column which carries almost no foreign matter in suspension and thus reflects perfectly the light that falls on it. Once the water breaks over the lip of the pool, it comes alive and is silent no more as it goes plunging down to the river. No wonder the Osages called this the Spring of the Summer Sky.

It is late when we climb aboard our boats again and push off downstream. But this is of less moment than if we were camping on our own and had all the chores to do when we reached our campsite for the night. Now we know Walter will have chosen a comfortable place to camp on the big, open gravel bar above Buttin Rock. He will have the two tents pitched and the duffle piled beside them. There will be a good supply of wood, and his cooking fire will be burning down to glowing coals. Beside it he will have set up the cot that serves as dining table, with its arrangement of slats unrolled on it to make a firm, flat surface. In the center of the red-checked tablecloth will be a Mason jar filled with whatever wildflowers happen to be blooming. And as the first boat comes into sight, on will go the coffeepot, kettles, and skillets.

Knowing all this, we take advantage of the dropping sun to cast at each shady bank, and between Ed's boat and our canoe we are rewarded with enough bass to assure a good fish dinner tomorrow night. Beyond this, we can unhook our catch carefully and release it or even put up the rods and drift along enjoying the beauty of the late afternoon. But Ginnie and Rick decide we should get to camp in time for a swim before supper, so we take both paddles and push briskly along until we glimpse the smoke of Walter's cooking fire.

On this first day out, which has been a long one, we enjoy supper to the fullest but afterward spend little time in spinning yarns. Instead, we lie back against our bedrolls to watch the constellations slowly circling the North Star and to count the falling meteorites, of which there are many at this season. Before any of us notice it, Rick is fast asleep with his blankets tucked around him; and soon we start to yawn and get the beds ready and follow him to the Land of Nod. Once during the night I wake to find the mist closing in and know that by morning it will drip like rain from the trees. But this happens on most late summer nights on Current River, and I turn over and am immediately asleep again —to wake when the aroma of Walter's boiling coffee-pot comes floating across camp.

Memories

Walter Martin cooks his pancakes two at a time so that they come hot from the big black skillet. A platter of crisp bacon, as many fried eggs as one's appetite can handle, cold grapefruit juice, and several cups of scald-ing coffee—all these combine to make a fisherman's breakfast. And as might be expected, it is Rick who sets the record for pancakes and honey.

We aren't in any great hurry today—yet are off down river by eight o'clock. Before we start, Tom and Ed make several runs through the fast stretch of water above camp, experimenting with lures. Finally they set-tle on a spinner-fly combination that seems to entice bass or panfish on nearly every cast, and with this they promise us a good day's catch, which turns out to be an accurate prediction. The fish can be kept perfectly

in the livebox that is built into the center of the fishing boats and gets its constant supply of fresh water from the holes bored in the bottom. If the fish are really striking, they can all be popped into the livebox as they are landed; and then from time to time during the day, the smaller ones can be released entirely uninjured.

As for us, we launch the canoe perhaps a half-hour behind the Cherbonniers, leaving Walter almost ready to start with his commissary boat. He will, of course, use his outboard motor and soon leave us far behind. There's an interesting story in connection with the name "commissary," which describes accurately enough the craft that carries the supplies. Our favorite river guide for many years—a wonderful companion and superlative riverman—was Garland Winterbottom, who was always called "Sairy" by the other guides. Garland was a great big, fine-looking fellow who stood nearly six feet tall and weighed in at two hundred pounds—and this somewhat feminine nickname was incongruous. Its origin, of course, lay in the fact that Garland had, for many years, been top commis*sary* guide for the Bales Boating Company. And even after he'd gone into business for himself and become a top outfitter on the Ozark streams, the nickname stuck.

The name of Buttin Rock, which we approach now, has also intrigued us—for it isn't "button," but "butt in," and there is a one-room school here in the river valley called Buttin School. Where do you suppose it came from? Could there have been some legendary Paul Bunyan whose name is lost today but who made it a practice to split the granite boulders along the river by the simple means of "buttin'" them head-on?

Not far below our starting point, Rocky Creek joins the Current. This, geologically, is an interesting small stream. It is known for its "shut-ins," or narrow gorges where the water has first worn out a fairly wide valley as it flowed over the softer rocks, then encountered the hard granite or porphyry and been so deeply entrenched that it could no longer change its course. In this case there is nothing left but to start wearing away the harder rock—and this the little stream does through the centuries, but slowly and cutting a very narrow channel. The "shut-ins" on Rocky Creek are now small canyons some fifty feet deep and no more than that in width, one of them spilling over to make a picturesque and imposing falls.

Far up on the head of Rocky we used to go turkey hunting in December, setting up camp for two or three days at a spring not far from the Norris cabin and then working out the big ridges and deep hollows with old man Norris and his boys as guides. These expeditions had come about through my acquaintanceship with Elvy Norris, one of the older sons, who had a little farm down closer to Current River and with whom I had quail and fox hunted on a good many occasions.

The first time we went in to the head of Rocky, which must be nearly thirty-five years ago, I am sure ours was the only car that had ever been over the last few miles of road. But old man Norris knew we were coming and had our campsite ready beside the spring and a good pile of firewood cut. We got there just before dusk and pitched the tent and built our fire. All the Norris boys —and recollection says there were five or six—stood in a line with their dad to watch, and finally I decided it might be well to offer a small libation in payment for

services such as wood chopping that had been cheer-fully rendered even before our arrival. This was back in the sorry days of Volstead, and I'm quite sure our supply of rubbing liquor consisted of grain alcohol in a couple of half-gallon bottles, part of it flavored with juniper berry and the rest with some concoction of Benedictine syrup that was sold in those dry times. At least it was so sweet it disguised the high potency of the brew!

Since we had a bit of genuine snake-bite remedy tucked away in the duffle bags, I wasn't too worried about the inroads that might be made on our bathtub gin and Benedictine. I told the old gentleman that if he would send to the house for a glass, I'd be glad to pour one. At once the "least boy" headed for the cabin and came back with a large jelly glass that I would guess held a pint. I filled it to the brim and handed it to old man Norris, rather assuming it would go down the line as a loving cup. But he upended and drained it with a single gasp, and it had to be refilled more than once as it went down the line. Not until it reached the least boy—who was all of seven or eight years old—was the amount poured cut by any noticeable quantity.

Next morning old man Norris and I were far out on Thorny Low Gap, having climbed down into and up out of a dozen steep hollows without finding sign of a gob-bler. We stopped for a breather, and the old man said to me, "You know, Len, I was plum tired out when you 'uns come last night. I'd been splittin' rails all day and couldn't eat no supper. But don't you know—after I had that snort, I went back to the house and had the old woman to fry me up some meat and potaters."

There is one other story I like to recall about the Nor-

ris family. They had originally owned a fairly fertile farm down in the river valley and then, with their half-dozen boys coming along, had expanded their holdings. But the farm depression of the early twenties caught them and they were sold out lock, stock, and barrel, down to the last heifer calf. If you will recall, this farm depression began about 1921 while the big boom in the cities was still building to its peak. The Norris family traveled up to St. Louis and ended in one of the steelmill towns in Illinois, across the Mississippi River.

There was no trouble about jobs then, and wages were good. With dad and three or four boys working, the family was making out fine. Except that they grew more and more homesick. Finally Norris and his wife remembered eighty acres that she had "heired" several years previously—a small patch of cut-over timberland on the head of Rocky Creek, with every acre standing straight on edge. The more they remembered it, the more homesick they got, until they could stand it no longer. So they pulled up stakes and went back "home." The first autumn they built a cabin for themselves and a lean-to shed for a pig, a dozen hens, and one cow that wintered on sprouts. By spring several acres had been cleared, and there was a vegetable garden and a patch of corn. The boys grew, and, while I wouldn't say the Norrises prospered, they managed to "make out."

I asked the old man, as we hunted together that day, why he had really come back. After all, four good jobs in industry bring in a pretty good income, compared with the four or five hundred dollars that could be scrabbled in a year out of this little hill farm. And his

answer I will never forget. "Sure, we got along all right," he said. "But do you know, Len, up there in the city a feller don't never see a sunrise."

Well . . . around the next big horseshoe bend as the river starts south again, we pass the mouth of Carr Creek and the ford just below. Here at the lower end of an island a doe and her fawn are playing in the shallows. This time it is clear no dogs are bothering, for they are unafraid and wait until we are almost on them before bounding gracefully up the bank.

Two miles farther along we come to Cardareva Ford and the big hole of water known as Log Yard. An old man is poling upstream in his narrow boat, and we recognize Tom Moss, whom we have known longer than anyone on the entire river. The valley widens out here for a distance of a couple of miles, and in this stretch of gravelly alluvial land Tom's bachelor son Ray has a fairly productive farm, though it is subject to overflow in time of flood. There was a long period of years when Tom himself guided on the river and was caretaker for one of the early sportsmen's clubs. Now he and his wife take things a bit easier—and high time, considering they celebrated their Golden Wedding Anniversary last year. They live with Ray, and Mrs. Moss keeps comfortable house for her "least boy." She is a fine woman— a real matriarch—and we are as fond of her and Tom as of anyone we know.

Another son, Ira, lives a mile or two down river at the Cardareva Club—which its owners and our long-time friends, the Jake Van Dykes, insist is properly named "Quo da Riva"; this being the supposed remark of some early explorer or other character (was he Spanish, French, Jamaican?) who found himself lost in

the region and asked (just whom he asked is not designated) in some strange language of his own, "Whither is the river?" This is, at least, the way Jake tells it.

Ray Moss is a good-looking fellow whom some mountain woman should long ago have claimed for her own. But he is modest and retiring and came home from the last war with no other desire in life than to live the rest of it in total peace on this little farm in Current River valley. Things aren't that easy, however, and today's trends in agriculture make life on a hill-country farm tough going. My hope is that Ray can stick it out.

Both Tom and Ira are more gregarious than Ray; and Tom especially is one of the really famous raconteurs of the entire Ozark highland. Yet this is hardly being fair to Ira, for when he really knows you and has come to feel that you are sympathetic with the hill people who are his neighbors, he can keep you rolling on the gravel bar for half the night with his stories. Even a few years ago when Ira was growing up, the back-country people had to provide their own entertainment and valued highly anyone with a sense of comedy. With no radio or television, few roads, movies a long way off and out of reach—storytelling developed into a fine art. Vance Randolph, who lives down in Eureka Springs, Arkansas, and has a mighty fine sense of humor himself, has been able to build several highly amusing books out of this capacity of the mountain folk for storytelling. Two of them are *We Always Lie to Strangers* and *Who Blowed Up the Churchhouse?*

It isn't easy to put one of Tom's stories down in writing, for most of their charm is in setting and delivery. The porch of an unpainted board cabin . . . a

campsite where a fire burns cheerfully beside a mountain stream—these are places where the tales sound best. Always they are about, in a broad sort of way, the very people who are listening to them: Tom's or Ira's mountain neighbors. And the laugh is with—not at—the fellow on whom the tale is told. This is why our storytellers want to be sure you are sympathetic; they will not have you laughing at their neighbors.

"Did I ever tell you about Cleve Bland and the cat's tail?" asked Ira one evening when we were camped on the head of Jacks Fork. We allowed not, and he went on. "You know, Cleve is a little, sawed-off feller and hard of hearing, but stout as a mule. One winter he was working for me in the woods, and I sent him away up on the head of Shawnee Creek to cut some white-oak stave bolts. You know, for makin' whiskey barrels.

"Well, Cleve went off up there and took his least boy with him and they stayed in an ol' cabin and I kindly forgot about 'em until Christmas Eve. That night there come a knockin' at our door, and when I went to open it, there stood Cleve and his boy with the snow blowin' around them and lookin' like they'd been dragged through a knothole.

" 'My gracious, Cleve,' I said, 'come in here by the fire and tell me what happened to you.'

" 'Well, you know, Iry,' answered Cleve, who talked in a ear-splitting shout as some deaf people do, 'We was up there in that goldurned little cabin, me and the least boy, a-splittin' them stave bolts and gittin' along real good. But the cabin didn't have ary door or window in it, and the boy tuck down with pneumonia, and up come a big snow and it aflyin' in through the cracks.

" 'There I was—a-firin' that stove with one hand and

a-tendin' my least boy with t'uther and the snow a-driftin' in, fer the cabin didn't have ary door or window in it. That went on fer nine days and nights, and finally on the ninth night I went to sleep a-settin' right in my chair. Hadn't hardly more than gotten three winks when the boy woke me up, a-hollerin', "Wake up, Pop, wake up, the cabin's afire!"

" 'Well, Iry, quick as a wink I woke up, and jest as quick I knew what had happened. We had a goldurned ol' cat up there in the cabin with us—and it a-snowin' and a-blowin'. I had th' stove fired up red hot, and the cat got under it and caught its tail afire. Next it run under the bed and caught the tow sacks afire. Tow sacks caught the bed afire. Bed caught the cabin afire —and there was the goldurn cabin a-burnin' down.

" 'Don't you know, Iry, it's a sight the houses that's burned down from cats' tails ketchin afire.' "

Of course I can't tell it like Ira tells it, and Ira can't tell it quite as Tom tells it—but the story somehow has the flavor of the Ozarks in it.

There's a big gravel bar at the up-river end of Ray's farm with a magnificent stretch of water running past it and a high, timber-topped bluff on the other side. It is one of those ideal places to camp for several days, and we try to get down there at least once a year. The best camp we ever had there, I think, was several summers ago when Rick was spending his vacation with us at the farm. On a memorable afternoon one of our favorite nephews, Pete Schramm from Burlington, Iowa, arrived for a visit of a few days. It was Pete's first time at Possum Trot and also his first real visit to the Ozarks. He drove up in a somewhat battered station wagon which had the appearance, on the inside, of a

gypsy caravan or an Irish tinker's cart. To list something of what was in it is to give you a pretty good idea of Peter, who was, that summer, some twenty years old and on his way to his master's degree in wildlife biology. The degree, incidentally, has since given way to a doctorate, taken under the eye of Aldo Leopold's son Starker at Berkeley.

Young Rick took one look at Pete in his obviously authentic ten-gallon hat (then glimpsed inside the station wagon such gear as a hunting bow, guitar case, a couple of gun cases, a spear-fishing outfit, a big western saddle, and sundry duffle bags, pack sacks, and the like), and we knew the eight-year-old had found a hero. Nor could we want a grandson to have a better one. The time of year, incidentally was late June, and Pete was starting on his vacation with parental blessings. By this circuitous route from Iowa he was headed, via the Ozarks, to visit his girl in Denver (she has since captured him), climb a peak in Montana, spear-fish in the Gulf of Lower California, and see the Sun Dances of the Hopi Indians in New Mexico on the way home.

Pete looked at our two saddle mares, grazing just across the fence, and asked as to their health. Fine, I told him, but they both need shoes, and our blacksmith hasn't shown up lately. Nothing to it, suggested Pete, and he would be delighted to tack on a set of shoes if I had them. This was easy, for I could supply the tools. Not necessary, answered my nephew—and forthwith pulled from somewhere in the station wagon a complete horseshoeing outfit. Best way in the world to travel through the West, he explained. Just pick the flossiest dude ranch, ask if they need any horses shod, let 'em get a glimpse of the guitar if they hang back—and generally

you have it made with good accommodations and wages as long as you'll stay.

That night Pete sang for us, with guitar accompaniment, everything from Bach to "King Bedbug" and a few compositions of his own thrown in for good measure. Early next morning we set out for Current River and a two-day camp at the Log Yard Hole on the Ray Moss farm. Three hours later we dropped down the precipitously steep slope of Cardareva Mountain and came to a stop in Ray's front yard. The family came out to greet us, along with three hounds, and we kept our old Irish setter as well as Tiger in our car in the interest of peace. We went inside to visit for a few minutes and found the house, as always, as neat as a pin although largely unadorned except for some plain furniture, Ray's deer rifle, the bright quilts on the beds, and the electrical appliances that came along with the REA power line to be Tom's wife's pride and joy.

I introduced nephew Pete as a fellow who could both play the guitar and shoe a horse, and Tom said he'd be glad to adopt him. Mrs. Moss is always mothering all sorts of creatures from children to foundling piglets, colts, calves, and lambs, but this time it was something different. She told Rick to come to the kitchen with her, and when they returned, they were followed by a beautiful little spike buck with a red ribbon around its antlers. It made the circle of the room, nuzzling everyone; and Ray said it had never offered to strike with its forefeet, as young deer just growing out of the fawn stage are said to do.

Our visit over, we drove the mile upstream past the little one-room Cardareva School and then to the river, where we were able to park on a high bank not far from

our campsite at the water's edge. Ray helped carry down the gear and left with an admonition that we would have to watch out for a litter of half-grown shotes that were ranging free in this area with the mother sow. They had become accustomed, he said, to visiting the gravel bar each day to see whether passing fishermen might toss them something to eat. With Mike and Tiger, the setters, it seemed doubtful we'd be bothered by pigs—but little did we know.

Pete and I placed the camp gear in the shade at Ginnie's direction and then pitched the tent while she set up her kitchen. Rick, already a good camper at eight, set out to carry firewood from the drift above camp and soon had a good pile stacked up. Thereafter we ate luncheon and lazed for an hour in the deep shade. Along about two, Rick and Ginnie and the setters decided for a swim, while Pete took his mask, snorkel, and flippers and set out to explore the bottom of the deep hole on the far side. He found it some twenty feet deep and the bottom pretty much a tangle of sunken snags and big boulders that had rolled down from the cliff during the long years. For my part, I set a big rock in the bow of the canoe to hold it down and motored a half-mile or so upstream to float back with the casting rod. But the bass weren't striking artificial lures, and later in the afternoon Ricky and I resorted to live minnows to catch enough for supper.

That evening at dusk the Moss family came up to camp for a visit—Tom and his wife, Ira and his wife and youngsters who'd come up from downstream in their John-boat, and Ray with his guitar. We built up a good fire and told tall tales and listened to mountain music until Rick pulled his bedroll over close beside us

and went sound asleep and everybody decided it was time for bed.

Just before dawn Pete woke and dressed and took off up the hollow behind camp to see if he could bag a couple of squirrels for a Brunswick stew. Soon afterward I rolled out and started the breakfast fire and then, as Ricky joined me, headed up the gravel bar to reel in the lines we'd left out all night and re-bait them on the chance we might catch an early bass. Soon I saw Pete running across the field and at about that time heard an unearthly cry from Ginnie, who had gotten up to tend the coffeepot on the fire.

Fearing the worst—panthers or rattlesnakes at the very least—Pete and Rick and I burst into a gallop to reach camp. "Look!" cried Ginnie, pointing up to the bank where we had parked the car with one door open so Tiger, the young setter, could crawl inside to sleep. The old fellow, Mike, had lately become crotchety and refused to let the pup come anywhere near the campfire. With morning and our stirring, of course, Tiger had come out and accompanied Pete on his expedition to the woods. But Tiger hadn't closed the door, and now, as we looked, we discovered the reason for Ginnie's screams. Sitting on the back seat of the car and peering contentedly at us through the window was a 120-pound pig. Another one sat beside him, and a third had gotten wedged on the floor between the seats and now began to squeal in a voice that put Ginnie's cries to shame.

Getting the pigs out was quite a chore. Thereafter Pete put blunt arrows to his hunting bow and hazed the rascals away from camp. To the dogs we shouted, "Sic 'em!" but our efforts here were in vain. Mike and

Tiger chased with a will, but they were just as likely to chase one straight across the cooking fire and into the tent as in any other direction. When a pig stopped, both dogs seemed nonplussed and might end up rubbing noses with it or running in the other direction with the pig in pursuit. It was a game, plain as anything.

Just as we were finally getting things settled down again and breakfast on the fire, Ray appeared with a big pan of piping hot biscuits his mother had baked and sent to us in the obvious belief that we were underfed. And so the two days went—over all too soon.

Another memory that this stretch of river from the Junction to Van Buren recalls to me is of Andreas Feininger's visit. Andreas, staff photographer for *Life*, was doing a story on the famous sport-fishing waters of America, an assignment which eventually carried him 36,000 miles. When it came to smallmouth-bass fishing, Current River was deemed first choice. And since Andreas and I had worked on several Ozark stories together, his editors wired to see whether I would help find the needed local color. My answer was that I would be delighted, and we set a date about a week ahead for his visit.

The first step thereafter was to contact our outfitter, Garland Winterbottom, at Eminence and arrange for two float trips. There would be an immediate one during which we would search out likely locations and a later one with Andreas to capture the actual photographs. Ginnie and I met Garland and Walter Martin with fishing and commissary boats at Powder Mill and started downsteam. I knew, of course, that what Andreas would be seeking was scenic beauty as it exists along

an Ozark river. Garland, on the other hand, could not conceive of a fish story in *Life* magazine without a picture of a fish. On the first trip, more to please him than for any other reason, we fished hard.

It was mid-morning on our second day out, in a fine piece of swift water just above Gravel Spring, when I dropped my fly along a sunken log that lay parallel to the bank in perhaps four feet of water. Often such a situation makes a fine refuge and hunting ground for a big bass, and sometimes as your lure comes floating past, he will follow it for a considerable distance, remaining well out of sight. Then just as you are ready to lift the fly from the water, he will charge out and engulf it. In the present case I thought I saw a dark shadow moving beneath the log, for the water was clear as gin. Then just as I decided I was wrong, out moved the shadow—a good two feet of him. There was no sign of hurry as he picked up my fly, which was, momentarily, still, but as he did it, I could heard Garland's gasp from the back of the boat. From now on, in the crystal water, the drama was plainly visible.

I arched my rod and set the hook vigorously, but this worried the monster smallmouth not in the least. Garland swung the boat for the middle of the river where it was still shallow but where I could play our prize with less danger of losing him under a snag. Ginnie, in the bow of the boat, put away her rod to watch the battle, and Garland whispered hoarsely that I would have to put on the pressure. But I had seen something disquieting as the big fish swam along parallel to the boat, and it accounted for the fact that he was not fighting frantically. The hook of my lure had not buried itself solidly in the mouth of the bass but had pene-

trated the thin membrane between lip and jaw. Already I could see the hole where it went through growing larger, and the only thing that kept it from falling out was the taut line and leader.

"We've got to land this fellow," said Garland. "It's the fish we must have when your friend comes out from *Life* next Monday. There'll never be another like him, and we can easy keep him until then in the live box."

"Not a chance," I answered. "See where I hooked him?" And all the time our boat drifted through the clear water with the fish moving alongside, some twenty feet away. "As soon as that fellow makes a rush our way and I can't gather the slack, he's gone. Try making for that gravel bar, and maybe we can beach him in the shallows."

"Whatever happens, that's the biggest bass I've seen on Current River for two seasons," said Garland. "It would be a good lick to land him."

Whether I took my eye off the quarry for a second or somehow relaxed the pressure of the rod, I'll never know. But I heard Ginnie exclaim and looked to see the big bass turn toward the boat. As he did so, the lure simply fell from the hole in his lip and sank slowly to the bottom of the stream—spinner, fly, and pork rind all plainly visible. The fish seemed hardly to know he had been my captive for several moments, nor was he excited at being free again. Slowly he turned upstream and swam, with undulating fins and tail, back toward his home under the sunken log.

Everybody heaved a long sigh, for smallmouth bass come like this fellow only once in a dozen years or so in our cold Ozark streams. Yet somehow my regret at losing him was no more than momentary. Perhaps he

will be there to strike again one day when we are floating this stretch of Current River, and if he does, he will
have added another inch to his already ample length
and girth. The following week Andreas came and, sure
enough, took not a single picture of fish or fishermen
but only typical scenes along this beautiful mountain
river where the smallmouths lurk.

"Here's Water"

I have, however, gone far afield from our float trip
with the Cherbonniers. On this journey we stopped for
only a few moments to visit the Moss farm; then we
pushed on down past Cardareva Club and the old Eaton
Ford, which, like most of the others along the Current,
is seldom used any more. Travel from the little valley
farms to store or school or church is no longer on horse-
back or by team and wagon. Today trucks climb the
steep roads out of the hollows to the highway, although
there are still a few one-room schools to which youngsters come on foot or by boat, poling up- or downstream
and across the river.

One realizes also, along this part of the river, that the
John-boat still plays an important part in the lives of
the hill people. They use it to visit their neighbors and
for the fishing that is part of the business of living.
Most of the boats tied at the landings are rigged with
some sort of light for gigging at night, although this
mode of fishing is limited to a certain season and to such
rough (non-game) species as suckers, red horse, and the
like. The method of fishing here is to have a powerful
light with some sort of reflector at the bow of the boat
which shows up clearly the bottom of the river in the

clear water. The fishermen, generally two or three of them, stand in the boat and are armed with spears of three or four prongs fitted to smoothly whittled handles perhaps ten feet long. A cord is attached to the end of this shaft for retrieving the gig. The spear itself is hand forged and is often of real artisanship.

The boat is run upstream to the point where the fishermen want to start. (Generally they go by outboard motor today, but in the old days the boat was poled by setting the gigs against the bottom of the river and pushing.) Then the light, which may be a gasoline lantern or a cruder gasoline torch, is made ready, and the craft starts downstream. Before the days of these artificial lights a board platform was built amidships in the fishing boat, and on it was set a crude metal-hoop basket. The platform was covered with several inches of wet mud, and in the basket a fire was built of pitch-pine knots gathered on the mountainside and replenished from a pile in the bottom of the boat. This made a fine fire that lighted up the river valley for a mile up- and downstream with a wavering, somehow mysterious light. The old "fire boats" before the day of the gasoline torch were special craft, very long and very narrow, and how the river folk managed to navigate them without constantly swamping and turning over has always been a marvel to me. How they ever manage to spear any fish even today is also something of a wonder; yet many of the rivermen are deadly with the gig.

This whole sport, which is practiced only by the people who live along the river or at least were raised here and come back to visit, is somewhat controversial. The natives fish for food as well as sport, although I'd hardly say food is still a real objective. But they claim they

should have the right to gig year-round and should not be penalized for the occasional game fish found in their bag. The more conventional fishermen, especially those from the cities who spend considerable sums to come to the Ozarks for sport, claim gigging is highly destructive to game fish and should be prohibited entirely.

The present status of gigging is a somewhat nervous compromise. The sport can be carried on legally in late autumn and winter and early spring. This is satisfactory because the streams are clear at this season. The quarry is limited to rough fish as already stated, and this is also logical, since expert giggers could literally clean out a stretch of river of all its game fish of any size. My own feeling is that gigging should be prohibited entirely on all the small creeks that cannot be floated by boat but that serve as our best game-fish hatcheries. A party of good giggers wading such a stream can kill everything down to the smallest sunfish—and they do it on countless occasions despite the game laws. On the larger streams where gigging is done from a boat, I believe that under present regulations it does not affect other type of fishing to any degree. Certainly it can be classed as a sport, and it is an exciting one that requires a high degree of skill.

When we come to Sugarcamp Hollow, after our visit with the Moss family, we find Walter's boat pulled up in the deep shade and luncheon ready. The riverbank here is heavily timbered, but the valley widens out beyond the timber to support a farm or two. Out at the far edge of this valley, perhaps a half-mile away, are several Indian mounds, almost lost now in the second-growth forest but undoubtedly remnants of a settlement of the early mound builders. Some day when we

are traveling the back roads of Shannon County with a jeep, we will visit and explore these mounds. But this day in midsummer is hardly the time—with chiggers and ticks and an afternoon temperature that promises to climb into the high nineties.

Down below Sugarcamp in early afternoon we pass Paint Rock Bluff, which gets its name from the odd coloring of the rock formation, then stop to fill our water jugs at Gravel Spring. Here we laze for a few moments in the shade where the air is cooled by the great volume of water that boils up out of the gravel bar . . . and I recall, as always, another one of old Tom Moss's stories.

It seems he was camped a mile above the spring with a party of fishermen one night, and they were just getting ready for bed when the valley lighted up and a fire boat came floating round the bend. The giggers evidently had a jug of mountain dew in their boat, as well as an unusually big pile of pine knots, and the fire in the middle approached the proportions of a conflagration. In fact, just about the time they came opposite camp, the embers falling into the bottom of the craft caught it on fire. One of the giggers at the stern, somewhat the worse for the fire water he had consumed, let out a shout.

"Hey, boys," he cried, "the boat's afire! Pole for Gravel Spring." At this moment his long-shafted gig caught under a rock in the river bottom and jerked him overboard. As he came sputtering up, an idea struck him. "Never mind poling for Gravel Spring, boys," he shouted. "Here's water."

This country that flanks the river on both sides below Gravel Spring for several miles is rough and rugged,

and the river flows fast to provide some of the best fishing water of the entire journey. Again the bird life is rich and varied, and I try to teach young Rick the difference in coloration, shape, and flight pattern of birds of prey that are common here. There is the turkey vulture—always black, soaring with seldom a flap of its wings, and with a distinctly dihedral tilt to the big wing primaries. The osprey shows white from underneath and is frequently seen hovering with rapid wing-beats before it dives. There is black at the elbows of its wings, which have a backward crook that plainly characterizes this big fish hawk.

As for the other hawks, it is enough for a youngster to begin with the groups. First are the harmless and entirely beneficial soaring hawks, or *buteos*. Red-tailed, red-shouldered, and broad-winged are commonest—all with heavy bodies, broad wings, and broad rounded tails —and we see them circling the sky in big sweeps. Next are the accipitors, or diving hawks—chiefly the Cooper's and sharpshin. These are hunters with short, rounded wings and long tails; they lurk in trees and dive at their prey. When flying we note quick wingbeats and a short, coasting sail. The beautiful little sparrow hawk is our only common falcon, although pigeon and duck hawks visit the river now and then. These are also hunters with long tails and long pointed wings which they stroke strongly and rapidly in flight. The prey of the sparrow hawk, of course, is chiefly insects, although he takes a songbird now and then. Finally is the marsh hawk, a harrier, generally seen hunting low over the meadows and with a slight dihedral or upward slant to the wings.

All this instruction in ornithology takes place casually as the various species present themselves, and this

is not frequently enough to interfere with Ginnie's fishing. But we had decided during the lunch hour that today we would make an earlier camp and allow time for a real swim before the air cooled off. Afterward, if it was still light, we might get in an hour's fishing above camp. So at three o'clock Ginnie puts up her rod, I spin the outboard, and we go zooming downstream. Though we are, on principle, against the noise and fumes of the outboard motor on wilderness rivers, I must confess that at times such as this it is a mighty handy invention.

It is four-thirty when we come down through the long stretch of quiet water oddly known as the Ant Hole and find Walter with his tents pitched and commissary department neatly arranged. Quickly Tom and I help him clean and scale more fish for supper, and afterward I join the rest for a cool swim in the deep pool in front of camp. That adds zest to the cold toddy and whets an already keen appetite for Walter's heaping platter of perfectly cooked bass, big black perch, and goggle-eye.

When supper is over and we've straightened things up, Ginnie and Adelaide volunteer to finish the dishes while Walter and Tom take Ed and Rick and me upstream a mile or so to fish back in the gathering dusk. Ed and Tom in their fishing boat turn back at the first rocky run and float through it several times, hooking and releasing more than a dozen big goggle-eye and a bass or two before floating into camp. Walter and Rick and I take the canoe a bit farther to try for a largemouth among the sunken logs that edge a deep, still hole. As Walter literally calls each cast, we hook one bass of good size and a half-dozen grandfather goggle-

eye. By that time it is dark, and we are glad to float back to camp down the rocky run and turn in under the stars.

Next day as we float downstream again, it is plain that the river valley is beginning to widen out. There are narrow bottoms on one side or the other that support small farms, although every mile or so the hills close in again and giant bluffs rise above us and the rapids are as rough as ever. They roar even more loudly because of the greater volume of water they are carrying. We stop at the mouth of Rogers Creek for luncheon, and Walter Martin recalls one trip we made some years ago when the weather did not co-operate as beautifully as it is doing today. On that occasion we were floating with Glenn and Lexie Hill and Myron and Muriel Northrop, who are favorite outdoor companions, being expert ornithologists and equally enthusiastic botanists. They had not, however, had much experience in floating the river. For this reason, although the Hills and Ginnie and I had our two canoes, we had brought along Walter Martin and one of his boats for the Northrops. Our gear was divided as equally as might be between the two canoes and the boat.

On the last day of that journey, at about ten in the morning, we were still several hours upstream from Van Buren, which was our destination. The wind came up until it was almost impossible to navigate, and we could see a severe storm bearing down river toward us. Since it was midsummer, when thunderstorms in the Ozarks are generally of short duration, we decided to find a high gravel bar where we could pitch our big tent, eat lunch, ride out the blow, and then push on again. Everything worked as planned, once we man-

aged to get a fire going in the driving rain, except that the storm didn't blow over. By the time we'd made coffee and had our sandwiches, in fact, the wind had risen to a half-gale and the rain came in sheets.

We decided finally that if this kept on, we might easily be caught before nightfall in a big rise that would make either camping or running the river not only uncomfortable but downright dangerous. So we donned all the rain gear we owned, struck the tent, packed most of the equipment in Walter's boat and took off for Van Buren. Fortunately Walter's fishing boat sported a motor, and this we put to good use. Two of the girls were loaded into my canoe, and the other perched in the bow of the John-boat. Glenn and Myron manned Glenn's empty canoe, which they could now manage even in the storm. We lashed my canoe alongside Walter's boat with a couple of hitches that could be easily cast loose. Walter gunned his motor, and we were off.

In every chute and rapid, we'd have to cut the canoe loose and paddle through; and even in the easier stretches we couldn't motor fast for fear of swamping, since both canoe and John-boat were loaded until they had little freeboard. The girls kept busy baling the rain from the canoe with the big sponges we carry for that purpose, and now and then Walter would bale his heavier boat with his scoop. The rain still fell in torrents, but the wind laid, and this made things easier. Behind us came Glenn and Myron, making almost as good time with their light craft and paddles as we did with the motor. We could look back and see them with Myron, who'd never paddled a canoe before in his life, manning the bow and digging in like a veteran. Now

and then in a long, slow stretch, we would get ahead and then round a bend and lose them for a while as we rushed through the next rapid. On such occasions I'm sure that Muriel was convinced she'd never see her husband again.

It was late afternoon when we finally made Van Buren, and the rain was still pouring down. It had been hours since anyone had boasted a dry stitch of clothing anywhere about them, but fortunately the day had stayed warm, and we'd had some exercise paddling and managing the towed canoe. While the men unpacked, the three girls hiked the mile across the long bridge to the old Rose Cliff Hotel on the far side to see if they could locate Walter's truck and our cars and also to reserve rooms for the night for the six of us. Walter, once his boat and gear were loaded, would head up the highway for Eminence, while we'd drive home on the morrow by a somewhat different route.

When Ginnie, Lexie, and Muriel arrived at the hotel, our good friend and proprietor Ben Davis had gone over to town for his mail. His cousin at the desk took one look at the three bedraggled waifs who stood waiting to register and allowed the hotel was full. Fortunately Ben's man of all work, Pete, happened along at this moment and said, "Why, Mrs. Hall, did you folks have trouble on the river?" That turned the trick, and soon the girls had located our cars, sent them across to where we waited at the gravel bar that served Van Buren as a landing, and were getting out of their wet togs and into blankets until we should arrive with the duffle bags and dry clothing. So the expedition had a happy ending; but the tale explains why, when a dozen middle-aged female schoolteachers want to rent two John-boats

and take off down the Current River for a float trip, I do my best to discourage them.

As for the present trip, we come down to Mill Creek, the little spring-fed stream that drains our own 1,200 acres of forest land in Carter County. Then since the good fishing water is mostly past and we are coming to several long, still pools that offer only hard paddling, we put up the rods and start the little Sea Horse. The bow lifts, and the wind in our faces has a pleasant coolness. Once or twice, coming to a rapid or chute where the river shallows, I tilt the motor and turn it off and pick up my paddle. Then when we come out into deeper water again, away we go. At four o'clock we reach the gravel bar above Van Buren where the boats "take out." Walter is already here and has his gear unloaded, as do Tom and Ed and Adelaide. The truck for the boats is waiting, as well as our two cars which had been driven down from Eminence since noon. Soon our duffle bags and tackle are packed, the fish are cleaned and iced, and we have changed to dry clothing. We're on the way home to Possum Trot.

# 10

One of the loveliest of the small springs in the entire Current River valley is located on Mill Creek, some eight miles northwest of Van Buren. Where the creek itself joins the river, there is little to distinguish it except its clarity during times of dry weather, for it comes in at the lower end of an open field that is bordered by a high clay bank. In time of heavy rainfall, however, Mill Creek comes pouring down in a brown torrent that probably adds fifty million gallons a day or more to the flow of the parent stream.

There is nothing abnormal about this huge run-off during time of flood. Mill Creek drains a steep, winding valley nearly twenty miles long and collects its flow from a hundred deep hollows that lie within its 25,000-acre watershed. There are many springs along this valley that once supplied household water for little mountain homesteads long since abandoned. These springs, taken together, have a total flow of four or five million gallons a day, and the only wonder is that Mill Creek runs intermittently instead of making a stream of respectable size throughout the year.

The reason for this is really no mystery. Here along Current River are small tributary creeks whose valleys are floored to a depth of fifty feet or more with accumulations of gravel and loose chert washed down from the hillsides. Such gravel beds have the local name "sinks." They are highly porous and take up not only the flow from the springs but also the rainfall except for short

periods following unusually heavy precipitation. This water which sinks down into the beds of these streams and disappears will eventually find crevices in the basic rock through which it seeps into underground reservoirs that may feed larger springs many miles away.

There are a half-dozen groups of springs along this particular valley that start the creek to flowing, but in each case this flow sinks into the gravel and is lost within a few hundred yards. It is not until the largest spring rises, perhaps two miles back from Current River, that Mill Creek establishes any permanent flow. This spring, in times of normal rainfall, pours out its million gallons a day of 55-degree water from beneath great moss-covered boulders at the base of a wooded hillside. As it tumbles swiftly toward the river, the spring branch supports a growth of watercress that would easily supply the restaurants of New York City. A mile or two farther up Mill Creek is another group of springs—much depleted in flow today—that used to furnish the water for a small gristmill and thus gave the creek its name.

Our interest in Mill Creek valley comes from the fact that we acquired here several years ago, as a family forestry project, some 1,200 acres of cut-over timberland that still supported a fair stand of seedling pine and small scarlet oak. The tract lies along both sides of Mill Creek and takes in the large spring just described. Of equal interest is that the land is bordered on its two-mile western boundary by the 25,000-acre Peck Ranch Wildlife Refuge where Missouri does most of its research on wild turkeys. Peck Ranch embraces nearly all of Pike township in Carter County and is managed by the Missouri Conservation Commission.

The area taken in by the refuge has a long history.

Much of the land was acquired in the 1890's by two brothers named Peck from Kansas who hoped to operate it as a sheep ranch. The forested ridges, however, provided little forage for sheep, while wolves and coyotes and an occasional panther took heavy toll of the flocks. At last cattle were substituted for sheep, and these were cared for in desultory fashion by squatters who had taken up residence along the narrow valleys and built their cabins beside the springs. These people ran a few cattle of their own, as well as hogs of the razorback type, letting them forage in the forest. They hunted year-round, took fish by any means possible, and in general lived off the country without active farming other than a small corn patch, garden, and a hayrick or two.

Apparently by the time of World War I the Peck brothers had vanished from the scene. They had lived here only briefly, and their heirs were scattered. Some of the squatters acquired dubious titles to their land; others merely continued to squat. During the war some surface iron mining was done in an area south of Peck Ranch, and the smelters of the Midco Company included a large charcoaling operation. As far as can be determined from the record, Midco acquired timber rights on the Peck property and skinned off everything that would make charcoal. During the years of this operation, it is claimed, more than 3,000 people built their cabins up and down the creeks hereabouts and worked in the timber or the charcoal kilns or the smeltery—and this in an area where not a single soul lives today. Even before the charcoaling, however, the land had been logged of its good pine and oak, either legally or by the process known in the Ozark hills as "grandmawing."

Like such other Ozark customs as gigging fish, hunt-

ing out of season, and setting fires in the timber, "grand-mawing" deserves an explanation. As in any forested country that is opened up to logging, most of the land surface of the Ozarks belonged to big lumber companies who bought the land outright for a few cents an acre or merely purchased the timber-cutting rights. The logging operations in their heyday employed most of the local population and even brought in other workers who, oftener than not, settled down on land contiguous to the forest. When the cutting and sawmilling was over, these people were left without means of support except to farm their barren acres, run some thin cattle and hogs in the cut-over woods, and salvage anything they could find in the way of saw logs. Being woods-runners by nature, they knew every nook and cranny of the forest, including the location of every marketable tree missed by the loggers as well as every young tree growing to marketable size.

The years went by, and the illegal harvesting of these trees from "company land" by natives who had formerly worked for these very timberland owners became a recognized hill-country occupation. The only difficulty lay in marketing the logs, and even this was readily solved. In order to maintain some semblance of legality in disposing of his logs, the logger is required to state at the sawmill just where this particular timber was cut—in terms of township, range, and section. The law has never been enforced very strictly, however, and in the Ozark hills until recently when you asked a woodsman where he had cut the logs he had just hauled to the mill, his answer was likely to be, "I cut 'em out on Grandmaw's place."

The U. S. Forest Service takes exception to the prac-

tice as far as their land is concerned. They have developed considerable skill at matching sawed sections of fresh stumps found on National Forest land to the ends of logs hauled to the mill, although the logger adds to the forester's difficulties by making a double cut. On state and private lands, "grandmawing" still takes place, and unless great care is exercised, the marketable timber disappears, tree by tree. The loggers use ancient and battered trucks that help give the Ozarks their name as an automobile graveyard. But the lights always work and are often supplemented by a powerful spotlight, since a good deal of illegal logging is done at night. The truck pulls off into the woods where one or more trees have been spotted. A gasoline chainsaw fells and trims the trees in minutes; and they are loaded aboard and the truck is gone, to stop at the next point where a marketable tree has been located.

There is, as with game-law violation in the hill country, an element of sport about "grandmawing." Yet now and then the practice is fairly profitable. There is at least one recorded instance of a timber stealer who, when the local authorities refused to prosecute him, was brought to the attention of the Internal Revenue Service. The foresters estimated his sale of stolen logs was great enough over a year to give him a taxable income; yet they knew he had filed no tax return. In the end, he was haled before a federal judge and paid double stumpage to the Forest Service for the logs he had "grandmawed," paid his income tax complete with fine, and spent a year in prison for income tax evasion. This made his sport run to a fairly high cost.

On the Peck ranch area there was little timber left to steal by the late 1940's when Missouri began to acquire

title to the land. Perhaps fifty squatter families still scratched a submarginal living from little eroded fields along Rogers and Mill Creeks, while cattle and hogs and even horses in large numbers roamed the valleys and hillsides. Few areas in backwoods Missouri have a worse record of misuse of the land. And yet, simply because the human population was spread extremely thin, the Peck Ranch area probably contained the best survival of wild turkeys in the Ozarks. They were, of course, killed in season and out by the native hunters despite the fact that all turkey hunting is illegal. Yet here was one of the basic requirements for a wild turkey population: an area of 15,000 acres or more with little or no permanent human habitation and few roads carrying traffic. Here, also, were all the conditions that made the area practical for inclusion within the public domain: low economic value—partly natural and partly brought about by misuse; a timber resource that would take so long to recover that no private owner wanted it; and, finally, a remnant of a threatened wildlife species that might conceivably be brought back.

It took several years for Missouri to acquire title to the solid block that today makes up the Wildlife Refuge. It was determined that though all the land would be put under management, not all of it need be fenced to exclude livestock. In the light of experience this was probably a mistake; but, at any rate, the refuge ended up with some 12,000 acres under tight stock fence and another 13,000 or so which lies outside and, except for careful fire protection and some improvement of the timber stand, is as badly abused by overgrazing as before the state purchased it.

As might be expected, the refuge program was not set

up without some resentment on the part of the mountain people whose cattle and hogs were eventually moved off of land that had supported them for more than a generation. This resentment showed itself chiefly in a fierce wave of incendiary fire setting. Then, as nearly always happens in these cases, the resentment—or much of it—died down. The refuge people were able, from time to time, to give employment to the few menfolk left in the neighborhood; and they used the refuge equipment to grade and gravel some of the almost impassable roads leading to the most isolated farms. Moreover, the population gradually declined enough so that grazing pressure was lightened in the surrounding countryside, and the remaining livestock did as well or better than before.

The turkey program at the refuge is chiefly interesting because it depends so little upon artificial means. Every effort is being made to improve the habitat for the big birds and then to leave them strictly alone to breed and increase. After four years the research program is well under way and shows every sign of succeeding. After the first incendiary fires, the record of fire protection has been excellent. In the 12,000 fenced acres—and in at least some of the bordering refuge lands outside the fence—the turkeys can travel their dozen or so miles a day as they range for food without being disturbed. There is a predator-control program but a great deal of doubt as to whether it is either wise or needed.

Management and research have gone hand in hand on the refuge, first under the direction of biologist Ken Sadler and later under that of Gus Artus. Management consists of opening up the ridgetops where turkeys like to feed and planting food patches in these openings; improving the existing small ponds often found on the

ridges and building new ones; fertilizing and seeding abandoned fields to food plants relished by the big birds; carrying out timber-stand improvement through girdling of cull trees and spraying, then allowing the openings to grow up in native plant species that furnish natural turkey food.

A remarkable thing about this program is the speed with which the habitat improves once the grazing livestock are removed and the area is protected against annual burning. In a short time the native grasses reestablish themselves, until now the big bluestem and such other nutritious species as little bluestem, Indian grass, and purpletop have taken over from the once dominant broomsedge. There is also a marked increase in the growth of native legumes which include something like a hundred species of lespedezas, vetches, clovers, indigos, partridge peas, trefoils, and beans.

For anyone interested in land-use, to stand along the refuge fence in midsummer where the growth on both inside and outside can be observed is a revealing experience. Inside is the rich growth just described, while outside the fence where domestic livestock grazes and hogs root in the overworked soil, the only remaining ground cover consists of sneezeweed, poor-joe, poverty grass, and brambles. Here is a classic example of land steadily beaten down in carrying capacity and receding through a succession of more and more worthless grasses, weeds, and shrubs. It is as though nature meant to take this land out of use and did so by growing these unpalatable plants so that there would be time to draw up new minerals from the subsoil and to create new layers of organic matter through the death and decay of many generations of the useless plants. Thus the land

would rebuild its fertility until it could again withstand, for at least a short time, the attack of man and his domestic animals.

The number of wild turkeys at Peck Ranch Refuge is on the increase without any resort to stocking with birds from the outside, which seems good evidence that they like the steadily improving environment. The increase in numbers is actually determined more by ear than by sight. Both young and mature birds are seen regularly by the refuge personnel; yet nests are rarely found. Indeed, there is no systematic effort to check nesting birds, since the hens may desert their eggs at the slightest disturbance. There are, in fact, few creatures to which the term "wild" more truly applies; and the best way to make an approximate count of the number of birds on an area is probably to listen to the gobbling of the male turkeys during the mating season.

There may be some infinitesimally small proportion of domestic stock in the Peck Ranch birds from crossing with tame turkeys that have wandered out into the woods from the mountain homesteads. On the whole, however, the strain here is probably as wild as will be found anywhere, and it is upon this wildness that the ability to survive very largely depends. In Missouri as in most other states that have had a population of native wild turkeys, extensive attempts have been made at restocking with partially wild birds raised on game farms. By and large—unless the turkeys can be intensively managed—these attempts have resulted in universal failure. Even when the "tame" element is kept to a very small percentage and the birds are raised in a semi-wild environment, these game-farm turkeys lose the capacity to survive in the wild. The ability to hide the nest, scatter

the young in the presence of danger, escape predation while ranging widely—all these are lost to some extent. Moreover, these birds seem to have a tendency to flock with the occasional bunch of domestic turkeys on the backwoods farms and are then susceptible to the common barnyard diseases that make turkey raising always a precarious business.

The density of wild turkeys in the Ozark environment is never very great, and already a program of trapping and moving the excess birds to other suitable localities is under way at Peck Ranch. This trapping is one of the most difficult processes imaginable, so that the capture and release in new territory of each pair of birds involves great time and effort. Several methods are used, of which the pole trap and the large net fired from an electrically detonated cannon are most successful. The trappers, of course, try to take more than one bird at a time, and one reason for this is that a sprung trap or a single shot with the net will "spook" the birds away from the area for several weeks. Considering that several weeks have already been spent baiting them into the area and getting them used to trap or net, it is easy to see what patience and care must be exercised.

We are not even sure yet whether all this effort and expense in trying to preserve the wild turkeys of the Ozarks will ever result in a huntable surplus, but this is only half the objective. The other is to prevent a magnificent species of game bird from vanishing. There is something hopeful in the very effort, it seems to me; some increasing realization that man is a fellow voyager, as Aldo Leopold put it, with other creatures in the odyssey of evolution. Thus we begin to develop a dim sense of the kinship of all living things; a desire to live and let live; a

realization that man's conquests are not the sole aims of the universe.

As for our forestry project along the steep sides of Mill Creek valley, it chiefly points out how far man still has to go in making an ethical approach to the use of land. We are desirous of rehabilitating this land: of rebuilding the layer of humus on the forest floor, checking the present disastrous erosion, and promoting the in-soak of rainfall. We would protect the young seedling trees of the desirable species that are native to this area and would promote the growth of the larger trees by improving the stand and protecting them from fire and damage by animals. If we are able to do these things, this land can become useful and productive again. It will do its small share to protect the Current River watershed against too-rapid run-off that causes disastrous floods. It will, in time, produce a modest yield of useful forest products. It will support its share of wildlife—of deer and wild turkeys, raccoon, squirrels, and other creatures.

The sorry fact is, however, that the Missouri law—and especially the law in the Ozark counties—says we cannot do these things, or can do them only at a cost that is prohibitive. Anyone can graze on our land as many cattle, horses, and hogs as he desires unless we fence the land and then patrol our fences to see that the livestock owners do not cut and destroy them.

The arithmetic of why we cannot do this is simple. Cut-over forest land in the Missouri Ozarks in the year 1959 sells at $3.50 to $5.00 per acre on the average. After 10 to 15 years of good forest management this land may be expected to produce an annual yield in the nature of $1.00 to $2.00 per acre per year. The cost of fencing our 1,200-acre track would be approximately $6,400, which

is nearly twice its going value or the equivalent of 3 to 4 years income after the land has been held for 10 years. In addition would be $300 or more per year depreciation and cost of patrolling to prevent destruction. Moreover, once the land was fenced, the risk of incendiary fire because of resentment would rise sharply. Thus has the benighted attitude of the Missouri legislature and of the open-range counties in this matter of grazing done much to destroy any hope for the economic future of the Ozarks—as bad forestry and land-use did much to destroy its past.

Despite these problems, we struggle along in the uphill battle to promote good forestry at Possum Holler. We have classified the timber tract as "Forest Crop Land," which assures effective protection against fire and theft. In co-operation with the Department of Agriculture and the forestry division of our Conservation Commission we have undertaken what is known as TSI work—or "timber stand improvement"—at the rate of 80 acres per year and hope to increase this acreage. Under this program, the cull trees—that is, the ones that are badly fire-damaged or are undesirable species—are girdled and allowed to die. This not only returns huge quantities of organic material to the forest floor as the trees decay but greatly promotes the growth of good young pine and white and scarlet oak by opening up the stand.

It had been our hope that, as long as the present law exists, we might carry out a research project on the actual effect of unregulated grazing on tree reproduction and growth, as well as on soil impaction, loss of humus, and run-off. The project could be set up easily at Possum Holler, because on the other side of the fence we have the Peck Ranch Refuge, a perfect control area where

grazing has been entirely eliminated. Sad to say, both large landowners and the state foresters hesitate to support such a project for fear of retaliation on the part of the livestock grazers, an attitude that has much to do with our failure to end this evil.

Most of our journeys to Possum Holler are made in spring and autumn so that we can avoid the scourge of ticks that is the curse of all the open-range country and comes very close to destroying its potentially great recreational value. To one who has never experienced this, the number of ticks is impossible to conceive. You can step into the undergrowth in the woods for no more than minutes and come out with your clothing literally brown with a solid coating of tiny seed ticks. This is, of course, just one of the several sizes in which this pest is ever-present. As one Ozark friend of ours put it, there are ticks of all sizes, including "throwing ticks." These are the very smallest size, which are grasped by their larger compatriots and thrown at you if the larger ones cannot reach you on their own.

In April and May and from October until late November, camping at Possum Holler is a wonderful experience. The density of human population here is in the nature of one family per ten or more square miles, so that you get a real feeling of being in the wilderness. You pitch your tent at the edge of a clearing within sound of rushing water, and after supper as the stars come out, a silence falls that you can fairly hear. Barred owls and horned owls start to call, and along about moonrise you'll hear wolf-music drifting down from the high ridges. Next morning, long before daylight, you are likely as not to be wakened by the snort of a whitetailed buck trying to make out the strange shape of the tent in the

mist or the gobbling of the wild turkeys as they feed across the abandoned fields nearby. All in all, Possum Holler may never prove a vastly profitable venture financially; yet it pays dividends in other ways.

 SOME VAN BUREN FOLKS

Except for Eminence, which is located eight miles up from the mouth of Jacks Fork and really isn't on the main stream at all, Van Buren is the first town on Current River in a distance of 120 miles from its headwaters at Montauk Springs. Originally it was a lumber-shipping and sawmill center of considerable importance, though it hardly compared with Grandin, some thirty miles farther to the southeast. Since the decline of the timber industry, it is the trading center for a small farming district and seat of government for Carter County. It has also been for some years a recreational center of considerable importance, headquarters for fishermen floating the river and for many tourists visiting the country of the Big Springs.

Ozark towns aren't built right on the stream banks, because these are not quiet "mill pond" rivers. At Van Buren, for example, a twenty-four foot rise in time of flood is not at all unusual; and this rise may come down as a wall of water that carries everything before it. Thus Van Buren is set back from and above the Current and is built along both sides of Highway 60, which spans the river here on the second bridge in this stretch of 120 miles. The first is at Round Spring some sixty miles upstream. Van Buren is a mountain town with one main business street and an old red-brick courthouse set in a yard shaded by maple trees. The low wall flanking the highway serves as a clubhouse and general meeting place for members of the male population not employed at any

given moment. Politics, fishing, timber cutting, fox hunting, farming—all these are discussed on the courthouse wall—and sometimes on Saturday you will find an itinerant revivalist preaching in the yard and singing hymns to the accompaniment of his wife's guitar. Whether many souls are saved, I've never felt competent to judge.

When I think of Van Buren, I often remember a story that Ira Moss tells when he is guiding us on the river. As in the case of the flaming cat, it concerns Cleve Bland, Ira's old friend and fellow worker, who has long since passed to his reward and wouldn't mind the story being told under any circumstances. Cleve, as you know from a previous chapter, was a notable character. He was deaf as a post and talked in a voice that carried across three ridges and two hollows. Though stout as a mule and twice as rugged, Cleve stood just under five feet five inches. Working, drinking, and fighting might have been listed as his occupations, indulged in about equally. He had several sons, and he liked nothing better than to brag on them.

So we come to a time when Cleve was working with Ira in the woods and they set out for Van Buren one winter afternoon with a truckload of whiskey-barrel stave bolts. These were destined for Ira's Uncle Ab in Van Buren who was a stave buyer and about the biggest man in Carter County. He stood six feet four inches tall in his socks, could lift a two-bushel sack of wheat with one hand, and had two boys both taller and stouter than he was.

It was late evening when Ira's truck negotiated the steep and slippery ridges and finally came out on the highway, and a freezing rain had begun to fall. By the time they reached town and unloaded their stave bolts,

four inches of slick ice had built up on the roads. Uncle Ab insisted the two men eat supper and spend the night at his house, pointing out that if they tried to go home, they'd slide into a ditch and maybe kill themselves. Nor did Ira and Cleve object, for to have started back would have been courting disaster.

While they were eating supper, old Cleve got to bragging about his boys. "Fine boys, they are, and real workers, too," he said. "Stout as mules and BIG. Why, Ab, they're bigger than ary one of your boys—but not near as big as me!"

The population of Van Buren is not much over one thousand; yet it makes up in friendliness and hospitality what it lacks in numbers. Like many other county-seat towns in the Ozarks, including Eminence in Shannon County, it no longer boasts a railroad. The steel from the last one was torn up in the late 1930's and was, according to legend, sold to Japan for scrap. The last of it was on the way across the Pacific at the time of Pearl Harbor, and I expect the rest was shot back at us.

It has been interesting through the years, as conservation has become a subject of importance and often of controversy in the Ozark hills, to watch the progress made in this field by some of our Van Buren friends. Across the bridge from town on a rise overlooking the river stands the Rose Cliff Hotel. This is a big frame building and is now closed; but it was owned until he died by old Doctor Davis, who practiced medicine and operated the drugstore in Birch Tree. Ben Davis, his nephew, managed the hotel for many years, and it was headquarters for salesmen who traveled this part of southern Missouri and for recreationists who came to see Big Spring or fish the river.

As the years went by, however, these guests became less important to Ben than another group who patronized the Rose Cliff. Back in the mid-1930's the U. S. Forest Service began acquiring the land that eventually made the Clark National Forest, and this brought a number of foresters to Van Buren on one mission or another. At the same time, the newly constituted Missouri Conservation Commission was building its personnel of wildlife and fisheries biologists, foresters, enforcement and field agents, and various other technicians. All these, as well as representatives of the USDA and the local farm-extension agent made the hotel their headquarters. I recall an occasion when I stopped here with Lyle Watts, Chief of the U. S. Forest Service; Chester Davis of the Federal Reserve Bank, who has a profound interest in resources; Forest Supervisor Groesbeck; Buck Hornkohl, who had charge of grazing on the forest and is an excellent nutritionist; and the local Forest Ranger. At other times our companions have been Bill Bauer, the botanist, and Dr. Julian Steyermark, who wrote the definitive *Spring Flora of Missouri.* A resident of the hotel for several years and our great friend was Thad Snow, plantation owner and philosopher from southeast Missouri who completed, just before he died in 1954, a delightful book of reminiscences called *From Missouri.*

Whether Ben Davis was a success as a hotel man, I could hardly say. But he did become through the years and has remained one of the most devoted and best informed conservationists in the Middle West. He started out by listening through the long evenings—because he couldn't help it—to discussions of resource conservation and management, problems of forest growth and the in-soak of rainfall, the damage done by fire and over-

grazing. Ben ended up by listening with whole-hearted interest and acquiring a liberal education in the process. He bought books, read them, observed in the field, studied. In the last few years he has taken over several tracts of forest land which he manages today as scientifically as any forester. He also owns a jeep that he doesn't drive and an Exakta camera with several lenses that he doesn't use to take pictures. Both of them are at the service of his friends who want to trek into the back country or make color studies of wildflowers.

Another Van Buren friend is Rip Burrows: farmer, profound philosopher, and the town's postmaster for many years. Rip has a head like a Roman senator and a twinkle in his eye like James Whitcomb Riley. His family came to Carter County in the early days, and he was born out on the edge of the Irish Wilderness—a name, incidentally, with a story of its own which is told in the next chapter. Then there is George Henson who not only edited the *Current Wave* for many years but wrote everything that went into it, solicited its advertising, set the type, and often as not ran the press, addressed the finished product, and delivered it to the post office. We sometimes find ourselves on opposite sides of the conservation fence from George but would never dispute his vast knowledge of Holy Scripture. In addition to these are banker Stan Cotton and lawyer C. P. Turley, both of whom are interested in farming and forestry.

One of the best guides and rivermen who ever floated and fished the Current is Dick Moore, who is mentioned in the opening pages of this book and with whom I've made a hundred expeditions. When Ginnie and I first started floating the Current, I said to Dick, "Now, here's a girl who shows every sign of becoming a real fly fisher-

man. But I'm not the one to instruct her in this art. It's up to you. Tell her—show her—and keep the boat where she can reach the shoreline with her fly." Dick did what I asked, and Ginnie became a highly proficient fly fisherman with a real fondness for one more Ozark native.

We have had countless adventures on lower Current River with Dick Moore, Dwight Terry (who was his partner for many years), and several other guides. Once after the quail season had opened, one of these boys and I loaded our dogs in his boat along with some grub and our camping equipment, and headed down river to hunt birds on the little valley farms. Now and then we would jump a duck from some slough or backwater to add to our bag; sometimes we flushed a woodcock at the edge of a swale where we were working out a covey of bobwhites. On the first night we camped on a high bank and, when the temperature dropped below freezing, touched off a big pile of driftwood that had lodged here during a high flood.

During the night I woke and saw that the guide had pulled his cot out by the fire and was sitting there smoking his pipe. "Too much coffee?" I asked; for you may recall the criterion for strong coffee along Current River is that it should not quite dissolve the camp axe. "Or are you worried about something?"

He confessed he was worried. A few weeks earlier on a Saturday evening in front of the courthouse, it seems, some tough stranger in town who was the worse for red-eye had threatened him with a big rock. He answered with the immediate reaction of a rough and tumble fighter by clobbering the stranger with a left and then pulling his knife. The fight was over, and nobody minded too much, for the town would be glad to rid itself of the

trouble-making stranger. But my guide had also imbibed a bit of redeye that evening, so the sheriff haled him before the prosecuting attorney who bound him over on a charge of assault. It was the knife, of course, that caused the trouble.

I told him, from my profound legal inexperience, that all he need do was plead self-defense. This was what he did, and he was fined a hundred dollars for disturbing the peace, paroled to the prosecuting attorney, and the fine remanded on a year's good behavior. For a long time, however, whenever he needed a knife he would have to borrow yours. This was something of a nuisance; but it was not as bad as the tale he told of a 10-point buck that jumped the fence at Big Spring State Park one day when he was squirrel hunting and attacked him with obvious intent to do him in. Having no knife, he said, there was nothing to do but wrestle the critter down by brute strength and awkwardness. He considered it downright unfair when Earl Kinder, the game warden, came along and accused him of catching a live deer out of season. The only trouble was, he said, that he couldn't let the durned deer go.

Another buck figured in an experience I had while on a wonderfully pleasant float trip with Ed and Bud Culver and their wives, this being their first time on Current River. As extra guides, Dick Moore had lined up a couple of youngsters who were long on river experience but short on knowledge of guiding. One of these boys came from a big family downstream from Van Buren that had been, as I recall, without benefit of a wage-earning father for some time. Dick not only wanted to help the boy out but knew he had the makings of a real riverman. And

Dick was right, for Red is one of the best guides working out of Van Buren today.

We hadn't been on the river long when I also found a way to help Red earn a bit of extra money. The boy had the most powerful and accurate throwing arm that I have ever seen. He could throw a rock heavy as a baseball farther than one would imagine possible—or higher, for that matter. He could also throw it more accurately and had been trained in this art by hunting with rocks. A squirrel in the highest oak tree or a cottontail on the move were easy marks for Red—and this is the solemn truth.

Moreover the boy knew his limits. "Bet you a quarter you can't throw over that sycamore across the river," we'd say. "Take you," Red would reply—and our quarter was gone.

"Bet you can't sink that Pet Milk can floating downstream in three trys," we'd say. "Take you," Red would reply. Then he'd bracket the can fore and aft with his first two stones and sink it with the third. On our three-day journey Red did quite well for himself, never losing a bet. He did, on one occasion, run our boat up on a sunken snag that nearly ended our journey. It took ten minutes of careful balancing and rocking to get us off without swamping in the swift current.

The other lad was a hunter and, in those unreconstructed days, an inveterate poacher and out-of-season deerslayer. Or at least so he said and pointed to a dozen or more notches on the stock of his .22 automatic to prove it. On the second afternoon out we had set the mouth of Buffalo Creek as our objective for the night, and this boy was paddling the lead boat. Somehow or

other—probably in order to try to bag a mess of bullfrogs
—I had borrowed his rifle and was coming along in Red's
boat, a quarter-mile behind. As the first boat swung into
the bay that marks the mouth of Buffalo, this boy and the
Culvers saw a beautiful little spike buck up to his belly
in the water and browsing on the lily pads.

"My gun, my gun!" shouted the young guide, forget-
ting he had loaned it to me.

At about this time we swung into the bay, just as the
little buck bounded up the bank and disappeared into
the timber on the bluff.

"Now, what would you have done if you'd had the
gun?" I asked.

"Killed that deer—sure as shooting!" replied the boy,
almost with tears in his eyes.

"And what would we have done with the meat after
dressing out a mess of too-fresh venison?"

"Sunk the rest here in the bay," he answered.

"And what if your old friend Ed Allen had come along
in his boat just as you were dressing it out?" For we had
seen Ed, the Carter County game warden, and George
Laun, the Refuge Manager, on the river during the afternoon. Just at that moment I heard the "putt putt" of Ed's
outboard rounding the bend, and in they came to beach
and join us in a toddy and visit for awhile.

"What about it if you'd found us dressing out a deer
when you got here, Ed?" I asked, after we'd unloaded
our gear and settled down to talk.

"Boy, wouldn't that have been something!" he answered. "Especially with all you write about conservation and good sportsmanship and all that. Of course I've
been hoping for a long time to get the goods on this lad
here, because I know about all those notches on his gun.

But I'd have hated to haul all you folks back to Van Buren and into court and spoil your trip."

After they'd left, Dick gave the youngster a good talking to, for he believed that if a fellow wanted to violate any game laws, at least he should do it discreetly and not in the presence of witnesses!

"The Good Old Days"

It would be hard to say that any one stretch of Current River offers better fishing than another; yet I think we would rate the three-day float from Van Buren to Doniphan, the trip we made with the Culvers, as the best for big bass. As to whether fishing was actually better in the "good old days," we are fortunate in having some honest records available. Several miles downstream from Van Buren, perched atop one of the highest bluffs, is the Carter County Fishing and Shooting Club. This club was established in 1888 by four officials of the Kansas City, Fort Scott, and Memphis Railroad, a branch of the Frisco, whose lines skirted the banks of Current River for many miles.

The chief purpose of the railroad was to haul lumber from the big mills at Grandin, West Alley, and other points in the area, and it was, of course, this lumbering that eventually came very near to ending the fishing. In the beginning, however, this downward process had hardly started, and the members of the Carter County Club and their guests made many successful float trips. There were a dozen upstream points on both Current and Jacks Fork to which boats could be hauled by rail and from which they could float downstream again to the clubhouse.

There are records of fishing success kept by members of the Carter County Club for every year from 1889 to 1940, and the best way to gauge what has happened to this famous bass stream—as to so many others all across America—is to set down the tabulation by decades. On this basis the average catch per man-day follows: 1889–1890 (first year), 14.2 fish; 1891–1900, 13.5 fish; 1901–1910, 7.3 fish; 1911–1920, 8.8 fish; 1921–1930, 5.9 fish; 1931–1940, 2.3 fish.

It is fascinating for the angler to pore over the old Current River Club records. Says one of the very earliest: "Left train at Birch Tree Tuesday p. m., Aug. 22nd and entered Current River at Mouth of Jacks Fork the morning of 24th. Floated to Club House arriving Sunday evening the 27th. Quit fishing at Van Buren Sunday noon. Fishing excellent and weather ideal all the way. Individual catches: Alden, 40; McFadden, 50; Horton, 41; Atkin, 18; Earle Smith, 32; Edgar Smith, 24. Total 205 fish."

Another report reads: "Caught 175 bass with about 10 grandpas 3 pounds each. Jacobs had two doubles, one 3 pounds and one 2 pounds. Mr. Logan caught largest bass of past 4 years—a smallmouth weighing 4 pounds, 7 ounces. Fine float and water fine." And another: "River high but had fine trip with (guide) Andy Pitman. Caught 69 bass, one jack salmon (wall-eyed pike). Jacobs caught a double consisting of two 3-pound bass."

Charlie Callison, formerly with the Missouri Conservation Federation and now secretary of the National Wildlife Federation, finishes his analysis of the Carter County Club records with these paragraphs:

"What happened around the turn of the century to cause the fish production of the Current River to decline

so abruptly? All the factors may never be appraised in proper proportion, but certainly the figures lend support to the theory that the removal of the forests with which Nature protected the Current River watershed was the major cause of depletion. The virgin pine was stripped from the Carter and Shannon county hills during the years from 1890 to 1905. The largest sawmill west of the Mississippi was turning out 285,000 board feet daily at Grandin. And removal of the timber, which was cut clean as if by a gigantic scythe, was followed by further abuse of the land. The hills were burned annually in a futile attempt to turn them into farmlands; over-grazing and the plow assisted in laying the land bare to erosion. Millions of tons of Ozark topsoil, and later the underlying gravel, swept down the hillsides and into the streams, destroying fish spawn and fish food and fish habitat.

"The good old days were good, all right, but it didn't take man long to spoil them."

 THE IRISH WILDERNESS

Place names are always interesting to us. They grasp at the imagination, sending us off into the realm of fantasy. Sometimes the origin of such names is fairly obvious, as in the case of Owl's Bend, Hard Scrabble, or Pulltight. Sometimes it is less easy to fathom, as in the case of Lick Skillet or Enough. The name "Irish Wilderness" is one of these last—a name to conjure with. Even the place is something compounded equally of fact and legend. It is a vaguely defined area of about 200 square miles lying to the west and south of Current River in the neighborhood of Van Buren. Yet despite the fact that we cannot put physical boundaries to the Wilderness and fence it, we do know how it got its name.

The story begins a long time ago and a long way off. During the 1850's a thin line of steel rails was pushed southward from the young but thriving city of St. Louis. The fur trade had passed its peak, and trade in other resources began to take its place. Freight still came down the Mississippi and Missouri from the rich agricultural hinterland for transshipment to the east and south. Packet boats plied the upper stretches of the river and the Ohio and made the run to New Orleans.

Now there was need to reach the interior country. Mines were opening all through the area known today as the "Lead Belt." At Iron Mountain in the Ozark hills was ore to be worked and hauled to smelteries at St. Louis. This was the day of the robber barons, when a railroad might start out as an empire builder's dream,

develop into a sound engineering project, and end as a speculator's nightmare. The line south from St. Louis, however, was sound enough. Eventually known as the Iron Mountain and Southern, it became part of the Missouri Pacific System.

While this railroad was financed by men like Jay Gould, the construction was done by a group of newer Americans. The hard work of swinging pick and shovel on the right of way, laying and tamping the oak ties, carrying and spiking the steel rails, was done largely by immigrants from the famine-stricken counties of Ireland. In spite of the expanding economy of a young and growing nation—and because there were few laws to prevent the exploitation of workers—the hardest jobs generally went to the latest arrivals on our shores. Thus the gangs of laborers who pushed south with the construction of the Iron Mountain and built their shanties along its right of way were mostly Irishmen. Whenever construction halted, they were left to scrabble out an existence by any means possible.

It was this situation that aroused the attention and interest of Father John Joseph Hogan, a young Catholic priest who was himself an immigrant. Forty years later when he was a bishop, Father Hogan published his memoirs, *On a Mission to Missouri,* and it is from this source that we discover how the Irish Wilderness got its name. Although his mission was at Chillicothe, Father Hogan preached in St. Louis in the years 1854–55, and it was here that he noted the hard fate of his immigrant compatriots; not only those who worked too hard for too little money on the railroad tracks and were then left stranded, but also those who were unemployed and existed in squalor in the slums of the city. He de-

termined to do something constructive about this situation if it was within his power.

One thing Father Hogan believed was that there would be a future for these people if they could be settled on the land. Realizing that the rich prairie and alluvial soils of north Missouri were far too expensive for the experiment he had in mind, he went exploring in the Ozarks. Here his journeyings brought him into the Current River country, perhaps as much by accident as design. But he did find land—cheap and plenty of it. He realized it was not of prime quality for farming but recognized that its forests of pine and oak represented a rich resource.

Apparently Father Hogan acquired title to land on both sides of Current River, for the first tract entered was 480 acres on Ten Mile Creek, which lies to the east in Ripley County. This was soon taken up by settlers, however, and a second area was explored. This lay to the west of the river in what eventually became Carter, Oregon, and Shannon counties; and again it was land richly timbered and with creek bottoms that offered possibilities for homesteads. Soon a wagon train of settlers were on their way to the new Promised Land. Each of the elders had been born in Ireland, and each had stored away a land grant signed by President James Buchanan.

Frontier life is never easy by the standards we know today; yet neither was life too hard in the land that became known as the Irish Wilderness. The forest here was mature and supported no brushy "understory" such as we see throughout the Ozarks today. A man could often ride his horse for miles through the big timber, down aisles that opened up endlessly between the trees. Bluestem and Indian grass grew in these

openings, furnishing the best of forage for the few domestic animals owned by the settlers. The settler who cleared a few acres each year, however, could increase his winter feed and the size of his flocks which flourished throughout spring, summer, and autumn in the woods.

Hunting, fishing, and trapping were primary occupations of the Wilderness people, and game was taken not only for food but, eventually, to sell along with the pelts at the trading post in Piedmont, a settlement some sixty miles to the north. There were, by the spring of 1859, some forty families living in Father Hogan's settlement: most of them Irish immigrants of the Catholic faith, but also a few Scotch-Irish Protestants who had moved west from the mountains of North Carolina and east Tennessee. Land could be homesteaded for 12½ cents an acre, and it was not too hard for newly married young people or late arrivals to make a start.

In the Irish Wilderness few real settlements grew up. Van Buren and the smaller village of Fremont eventually were located on its northern edge, with Alton on the Eleven Point River to the southwest and Doniphan to the east. In the heart of the Wilderness was the tiny village of that same name, complete with one store that also served as post office. Over near Big Barren Creek, which the natives call "Big Bar'n," was probably the smallest post office in the country. This was at Handy, and it occupied a six by nine slab building where business was conducted until a very few years ago by Mrs. Catherine Probst, whose family was the only one located here.

Although life in the Irish Wilderness was not especially easy, it was good because it was essentially uncomplicated and little affected by the outside world. It

might have run along for many years; yet in the end the events of this outside world disrupted the Wilderness. For a time after the outbreak of the Civil War, little word of the conflict came to these isolated people; nor did they have reason for the intense feelings that disturbed the rest of the United States. But finally there was marching and countermarching as first Union and then Confederate troops occupied the Ozark counties.

Even troops, however, were not as bad as the bands of brigands and guerillas who now overran the isolated back country. These frontier desperadoes were given the name "bushwhacker," and they raided civilians regardless of affiliation with North or South. Livestock was stolen and driven off, granaries looted, houses burned. Doniphan was attacked and partially destroyed by the bushwhackers. Gradually the Irish people, who had no real part in any of this and no means of protection in their isolated situations, began to move away. Some of the young men joined the armies and fought out the war. Families left their ruined farms and settled in surrounding towns.

One of the youngsters who left to fight with General Marmaduke's Confederate forces was Billy Griffin from Ireland, who had come to the Wilderness as a young lad with his father. But Billy returned to the land that had been deeded his parents in 1854, and here on Big Barren Creek, where we hunt deer each autumn, he built his farm and lived to a ripe old age. Legend has it that, among his philanthropies, he gave land for the building of a church, with the understanding it was to be open to all faiths except the Mormon.

Much of our knowledge of the Irish Wilderness comes to us from our friend E. W. Burrows, men-

tioned in a foregoing chapter as a Carter County philosopher and postmaster of Van Buren. Rip Burrows
comes by *his* knowledge of the Wilderness at first hand,
for he was born on the edge of it. His own great-grand-
fathers helped settle it, having come here from Tennessee in 1849 with a deed to a grant of land signed by
President Zachary Taylor. And his step-grandfather
was this same Billy Griffin who lived on his farm on Barren Creek and finally died in Van Buren in 1917.

Father Hogan, writing long after the dispersal of
these people and doubtless sad at the failure of his effort, set down these words: "Who now will build up
these waste places? Who now will lead back the scattered settlers to their humble but ruined homes? Who
will rekindle for them the light of faith or preach the
word of God to them in their little chapel beneath the
pines of the forest?"

The day that Father Hogan hoped for cannot come
again. Most of the descendants of his people have perhaps found a life richer even than that in the Irish
Wilderness. As for the land, it was never meant for in-
tensive use by any large number of human beings. Today much of it lies within the boundaries of the Missouri National Forest and is protected against the fires
that ravished it annually for almost a century. The little
eroded fields are healing slowly and going back to
forest and bluestem grass again, while tall pines grow
on the north slopes of the hollows and oaks on the drier
southern situations. In Peck Ranch Wildlife Refuge the
deer browse safely and the wild turkey ranges widely
in search of food. Perhaps this is the best and wisest use
we can make of the land called The Irish Wilderness.

13 BIG SPRING TO DONIPHAN

There is no lovelier time of the year to be afloat on an Ozark river than late September. The heat and drought of summer have passed, and autumn flowers are starting to bloom along the banks. The beautiful cardinal lobelia appears, and great clumps of lavender bergamot as well as a handsome tall-stemmed meadow phlox. At the time of the autumnal equinox it is still warm enough to swim, although the days are seldom unpleasantly hot and the nights have grown markedly cooler. Twilight comes earlier, too, and one must make camp by five o'clock to avoid being caught by darkness before the chores are finished. Often at this season we round a bend to put a band of wild ducks to flight: sometimes the blue-winged teal and sometimes pintails or other early migrating species. Doves come in small flocks to the gravel bars to fill their crops with sand. Killdeers are gathering for the annual flight southward, and this is the season when we see whole families of the wading birds: little blue herons with their first-year youngsters still in white plumage, immature wood ibis, great blue herons, American egrets, and now and then a snowy.

We floated from Van Buren to Doniphan on the lower river in late September in a week of fine weather. The distance of some forty-five miles is a good three-day journey by canoe; and when Ginnie and I completed it, we had navigated a full 130 miles from Cedar Grove on the headwaters of the parent stream and an additional sixty miles or so on tributary Jacks Fork. On the present

trip we were anxious to get color movies of camp and canoeing scenes for our film *An Ozark Anthology*. And since one cannot conveniently take pictures of himself shooting rapids or cooking supper, we had persuaded Charles and Marian Guggenheim to join us on a busman's holiday. Charles has produced, during recent years, some of America's finest documentary films; and though he is not primarily a cameraman, he can, as might be expected, still compose a good sequence on his Cine Special.

The truth is, we had been planning this trip all summer long, and our party also included Leo and Kay Drey, whose Ozark interest centers in their great tract of forest land. Like ourselves, Kay and Leo and Charles and Marian are all canoe enthusiasts. They are also congenial companions, and we were delighted to have a three-canoe flotilla for this leg of our Current River journey.

On the day of our start the Guggenheims came to the farm for luncheon, with their gear and canoe packed inside and atop their station wagon. The Dreys had gone on ahead in order to attend a conference at the U. S. Forest Service headquarters in Ellington. As soon as luncheon was over and we had lashed our own canoe atop the car and packed the tent and other equipment inside, we took off down Highway 21 for Van Buren, which was to be our starting point. Since Leo and Kay would be late and couldn't join us before morning, we had agreed that we would take our two canoes and push downstream in the late afternoon to make camp near the mouth of Elm Spring Hollow, eight miles below town. The road from Van Buren through Big Spring State Park winds on down the river and touches at Elm

Spring so that the place can be reached by car. Here the Dreys were to launch their canoe next morning and start looking for us.

Eight miles was too great a distance to float in the short time left between our arrival in Van Buren and darkness, so we got hold of Flynn Dorris and "Doodle" Hildebrand, who often take care of the cars while we are on the river, and drove the four miles of good highway to Big Spring. Here we borrowed the Park boat dock long enough to set the two canoes in the water and load our gear aboard. We made arrangements with Doodle and Flynn to meet us three days later at noon or thereabouts at the boat landing in Doniphan with the empty cars. Then Marian and Ginnie took their places in the bow of each canoe, we whistled Tiger aboard our boat to his place amidships, and were off.

Big Spring's half-billion gallons of cold, blue water make a small river on their own, tumbling a half-mile down to the main stream. After the spring has joined the river, one can trace it for a mile or so by its light blue color. It swells the volume of the parent stream noticeably but is finally lost in it without a trace, blending with the darker blues and greens.

The character of Current River changes very little in these lower reaches. It is larger, and the valley widens out somewhat; yet the stream flows here through some of the wildest and roughest land in the eastern Ozarks. One thing we do notice is that the river becomes more of a highway than ever for the people who live along the valley. Powerful outboard motors are practical on the big 24-foot John-boats, and this makes it possible to travel upstream as well as down if you are an extremely skilled navigator. If not, it is easy to tear the bottom out

of a boat and lose it completely in any of a hundred chutes and rapids. Each farm we pass, however, has a boat landing, and many of the boats tied up along the river are rigged for spearing fish at night with powerful gasoline torches and long-handled gigs.

In everything except intimacy—the closeness of the timbered shoreline where one may glimpse a mink or fox squirrel, the clay bank where kingfisher and bank swallow nest side by side, or the pool where big bull-frogs hide at the water's edge—this lower river is as beautiful and as interesting as any other stretch. Now one may glimpse mistletoe in the tall sycamores and find wisps of Spanish moss clinging to gnarled cedars that are a century or more old. There are the same giant bluffs, often standing two hundred feet or more above the level of the river but now occasionally set back from the bank because of the greater width of the flood plain, instead of coming down sheer into the water. There are also the same clean, high gravel bars ideally located for camping. The river is as swift, and the rapids and log-filled chutes take as much skill as ever to navigate, since, if anything, the power of the current increases with the size of the stream.

On this first evening we had only about four miles to float from Big Spring to Elm Spring Hollow, where deer often cross in the shallows to head out along Bee Gum Ridge that runs away to the north. But by the time we passed the opening where the hollow meets the river, it was almost dusk, and we knew we must find our stopping place soon or make camp in the dark. So we dropped swiftly down past big Chilton Bottom and the Chalk Bank to the first small gravel bar, and here we pulled ashore.

This bar was not as high as I'd have liked; yet there seemed no chance whatever of any big rise coming down from upstream during the night. Moreover, a fine swift-water run flanked the gravel bar to keep the air moving and discourage mosquitoes. Soon the gear was set ashore, the canoes pulled out and overturned to drain dry, and everyone was at work on the camp chores. While Charles collected driftwood and started the cooking fire, I pitched the tent. Ginnie and Marian prepared supper to the point where I could come broil the steaks. In almost no time the meal was under way.

Twilight is short at this time of year. As we ate, we watched a flight of bullbats, as the nighthawk is commonly called in the Ozarks. This bird is, of course, no bat at all, but a relative of the whip-poor-will and a member of the goatsucker family. It takes its food entirely on the wing and, like other members of the clan, has small, weak feet which are ill-adapted to perching. It also has a tiny bill but an out-sized mouth that serves it well as it hunts for insects through the evening sky. Its wings are canted back at the elbow like those of some fighter planes, a characteristic which was immediately noted by our eight-year-old grandson, Ricky. It has another interesting characteristic that gives it the scientific name *Chordeiles virginianus;* this being its odd habit of diving from a height of several hundred feet and checking this dive suddenly so that the wing-primaries give out a strange booming as though one had struck a chord on the strings of a cello.

By the time we'd finished supper and dusk had deepened, the bullbats disappeared, and now the true bats came from their caves in the limestone bluffs to harvest insects over the water. There are a dozen species

of these interesting and valuable little flying mammals in the Ozarks, but since they seldom come out until twilight, it is hardly possible to identify them on the wing. The river bluffs furnish an ideal habitat for them, with countless caves and crevices and an ample food supply from the insects that hatch each evening.

Once darkness had fallen, we lit the propane lantern that operates from a small metallic cylinder. This flooded the campground in a white glow that attracted countless mayflies and other winged creatures; but soon the dishes were done, the food and supplies stacked snugly away and covered with a tarpaulin against the night dew, and the lantern extinguished. Then because we hadn't spent a long day on the river and were not especially tired, we built up a big campfire and sat back to watch the moon rise. Charles told of his adventures shooting wildlife film in Alaska, and we dug up an amusing tale or two about the things that can happen to Audubon Screen Tour lecturers when they are on the road. Tiger dozed beside the fire, and a barred owl came down out of the hollow to hoot a serenade. Slowly the campfire embers died to a crimson glow.

When bedtime came, since the sky was still clear, we blew up the air mattresses and spread our bedrolls on another tarpaulin outside the tent beneath the stars. At this season a heavy mist almost invariably forms along the Ozark valleys at night. On this night it was so heavy that once or twice when I woke, I wondered if it was raining. Always, however, the pale moon shown through the cotton-wool blanket that made even the river invisible, not fifty feet away. When morning came, mist still dripped in a steady downpour from the trees, and we were afraid the sun had deserted us for good. I

made the fire with difficulty, for even the kindling was dew-soaked. But soon the coffee was boiling and a big pan of bacon sizzled on the fire. I called my companions then, and only the prospect of breakfast finally got them going.

After the dishes were washed, we stoked the fire again before starting to pack our duffle; for Leo and Kay were due at any moment, and I was pretty sure they would not have eaten. And sure enough, just at seven o'clock their canoe appeared out of the upstream mist like a phantom floating on unseen water. They had spent the night in Van Buren, gotten Flynn to drive them to Elm Spring, and launched out with some misgiving that they might miss us in the fog. Soon a second breakfast was under way—with the cook's compensation an extra cup of coffee.

We made it a point on this morning to work out an even distribution of our gear and to divide the food between the three canoes so that, in the unlucky event of a spill, we'd still have something left to eat. Many a Current River float trip has come to a sudden and untimely end when the commissary boat swamped in some swift chute and sent the supplies to the bottom. And our precaution on this occasion proved a wise one, for not all of the supplies arrived safely at their final destination.

Once the canoes were evenly loaded, I rigged Ginnie's fly rod and laid my own bait casting rod along the stern thwarts, for neither the Dreys nor the Guggenheims are anglers, and they were counting on us for at least one mess of bass, goggle-eye, and sunfish. We agreed to keep fairly well in touch during the morning and eat luncheon somewhere above Panther Spring and the

mouth of Bear Camp Hollow. This would leave an easy afternoon's run to Gooseneck, an ideal spot to camp.

On this morning's run, Charles and I both kept the movie cameras handy. He gave Marian the responsibility of the stern paddle and mounted his Cine Special on a tripod set between his legs in the bow of the canoe. My Bolex was equipped with its gunstock and kept ready beneath a plastic covering just ahead of the stern thwart. This readiness is essential, since one never knows when a picture will present itself. Our progress was slowed, moreover, when on several occasions we disturbed an osprey from its perch in some dead snag or put up a great blue heron. With all this gear aboard, Ginnie and I took no chances of swamping our canoe in the rough spots; we negotiated them with the stern line. Leo and Kay, whose load consisted chiefly of their personal gear and a share of the camp equipment and food, ran all the small chutes and swift runs for the sport of it.

It is interesting how place names change as one floats downstream. Here on the lower river the quiet stretches are no longer small deep pools but often extend for a mile or more. Thus the Ant Hole and Log Yard Hole now become Gun Bay or Hargus Eddy. A place well named is the Cataract, a mile-long run of swift and treacherous water where the skeletons of great sycamores washed down in the floods of many years have lodged to lie in wait for the unwary boatman.

It wasn't the Cataract, however, that caused our only disaster of the trip. Along toward mid-morning, well above Panther Spring, our three canoes had gotten strung out over a distance of perhaps a mile, with Leo in the lead and Charles coming along behind us. We

rounded a bend at the lower end of an eddy, ran down a swift gravel riffle, and beached when we found Kay and Leo waiting at the head of a rocky rapid down which the water boiled angrily. It didn't appear too difficult to negotiate once you'd gotten properly into it and straightened out for the run. The trouble lay in the turn at the head of the rapid, where water from the riffle plunged precipitously into the bank at right angles, then swept down under the low overhanging limbs of trees that were no more than two feet above the surface.

Ginnie and I decided the better part of valor was to use the stern line and walk the canoe along the near bank until the current straightened out again. Even then, there were hidden boulders that piled up three-foot waves and enough ledges and sunken logs to make the rest of the rapid a thrilling ride. We negotiated the bad turn without difficulty, Tiger and Ginnie got aboard, and I swung the bow into the current and stepped into the stern. Once I looked back to see Leo's canoe shooting the riffle and apparently making the bend into the rapid successfully. But then I had to give all my attention to our own canoe, which was rushing along like an express train.

Just as we reached the roughest part of the rapid, I heard a shout and again took a chance on looking back. At first, all I could see was Leo's canoe coming down empty a quarter-mile behind and riding low in the water. Then beside it I made out Leo's head bobbing along, and it was plain he had a hand on the gunwale; but there was no sign of Kay. At last I saw her, clinging to a limb that bobbed up and down in the very heart of

the rapid, perhaps a hundred yards upstream from Leo and the waterlogged canoe.

What had happened was plain. In some manner Leo had let his craft be swept beneath the overhanging limb, and Kay had instinctively reached for it. The power of the current had simply snatched her out of the canoe, tipped it enough so that Leo also went overboard, and half-filled it with water but without turning it completely over. The only thing we could not figure out was why Kay, who is a good swimmer, hadn't let go the limb and come on down with Leo and the canoe.

There was a reason why she remained clinging to her bobbing branch, and, when we found it out, it made her into quite a hero. This did not seem the time, however, to try to surmise what the reason was. Instead, I swept our canoe into the slower water at the end of the rapid so we could head upstream again on a rescue mission.

Ginnie and I swung our canoe inshore, hauling aboard various items of gear from Leo's boat as they came floating past. At the same time, he worked his waterlogged craft in beside us, and we left Ginnie to tend his boat while we headed upstream to rescue Kay, who was still clinging to her tree limb and bobbing up and down in the current. With Leo at the bow paddle and the motor wide open, we worked our way swiftly up the quieter water along the shore, but by the time we arrived at the rescue point, Charles and Marian had also gotten there.

Now we learned why Kay had stayed there all this time, instead of simply letting go and swimming with the current until it carried her out into shallow water. When the overhanging limb swept her overboard, our

tent which had been spread over the load in the canoe went along with her. And Kay, realizing that if it once became water-soaked it would sink and be irretrievably lost in the deep rapid, had simply grabbed it. But once she'd done this, she could not let go her hold on the limb without having the weight of the heavy tent sweep her under. So with at least a fair amount of confidence that someone would be along presently to rescue her, Kay hung on until help came.

A few moments later we had all three canoes beached on the gravel bar at the foot of the rapid and were assessing the damage. As it turned out, the swamped canoe had righted itself so rapidly that little had spilled out except Kay, Leo, and the tent. All the gear from their load was immediately spread out to dry in the hot sun, the Dreys put on their swimming suits for the lunch hour, and, aside from a few items of perishable food and one small camp axe, nothing was actually lost.

Yet this was at least partly luck. If the canoe had turned completely over instead of righting itself; if Kay hadn't been level-headed and a good swimmer; if Leo hadn't known this and had enough confidence in her to go after the canoe first and ride it ashore; if the other canoes had both been a mile behind and so unable to help out—any of these "ifs" might have spelled the loss of a lot of equipment or worse. Not every boat that swamps in Current River comes out so fortunately.

In the end, our own upset caused nothing more serious than the loss of the extra hour we took to dry out the equipment. We used this hour to eat our luncheon and take a swim, and we found we were no more than two miles above Panther Spring where we

had planned on arriving at noon or thereabouts. But we decided we would like to reach our campground at Gooseneck at a reasonable hour, so it wasn't long before we took off downstream again. Thus we floated without incident past Stillhouse Hollow and Kelly Bay, where I once bagged a four-point buck on a rainy December morning at the very end of the deer season.

Except for the open land in the alluvial plain, the watershed on both sides of the Current from Panther Spring all the way to Doniphan lies within the boundaries of the Missouri National Forest. At Gooseneck, a gravel road runs down to the west bank of the river, and here a modest campground is maintained by the Forest Service. This is a satisfactory enough place in late autumn after the frost has killed off the chiggers, but in midsummer the big gravel bar on the opposite bank makes a far more satisfactory campsite. This bar covers perhaps fifty acres and is piled up to a height of twenty feet above the water, which gives some idea of the amount of gravel erosion that occurs on these Ozark streams.

Although the hills and hollows that flank the lower Current River are rugged in the extreme, they grew good timber in the early days, and now, under the management of the U. S. Forest Service, the trees are starting to grow again. Over to the east a half-dozen miles lies Grandin, today a sleepy village nestling between the North Prong and Middle Fork of Little Black River which joins the Current below the Arkansas line. There was a time, back at the turn of the century, when the great circular saws whined and sang in the Grandin mills that for several years turned out more lumber than any in America. Logs of pine and oak

came to these mills from the entire Current River and Jacks Fork watershed and from that of the Little Black as well. Narrow-gauge tram lines along the rivers and up the steep hollows brought logs to the main line of the railway that served the mills at Grandin, and the rights of way of these tram lines can still be found winding through the woods or following the banks of the streams.

This area along the Current was one of the first to be acquired by the federal government when our National Forests were established in Missouri, and it is here that some of the first work was done on timber-stand improvement. As openings were created in the cut-over forest by the removal of old cull trees and some of the useless brushy species, many interesting things happened. First of all, the growth of young trees doubled as the sunlight reached them and they were fed by the organic matter returned to the soil by the decay of the cull trees. Then plants reappeared that were relished by deer, and the number of whitetails took a sharp upward climb. This became one of the first areas where an increasing deer population actually made a hunting season necessary in order to remove the surplus.

We came to the big gravel bar opposite Gooseneck at about four o'clock, in plenty of time for a swim and a bit of live-bait fishing with minnows in the deep run in front of camp. Across from us, a small tributary called Spring Creek made a deep bay where it joined the river, and here, not long after we had beached the canoes, a band of fifty blue-winged teal came to a landing. We pitched our tent, for there were clouds in the west, and afterward it wasn't long before we had three chickens sizzling in the big skillets on the fire.

Early next morning Charles and I took the cameras and an empty canoe and pushed across to the bay where the teal had landed, but we found them gone. A great blue heron, disturbed at his fishing, took wing up the bay, and we beached and got out to try a stalk that resulted in a good shot or two before the big bird grew alarmed and took flight. Pushing farther through the growth of small willows we came to a marshy opening much used by the wading birds. Here countless deer tracks crossed in every direction, and masses of cardinal lobelia added beauty to the wild scene.

We were late getting under way, that morning, for the day's float down to the mouth of Buffalo Creek where we would camp was not too strenuous. Just below Gooseneck is the lodge owned by the Wright and Burford families of Doniphan where I've spent many a pleasant deer season. But this was mid-week, and the place was deserted. Thereafter we dropped down through an alternating series of swift rapids and long, still pools: Bay Nothing and Jakes Bay and Mayberry Bay at the mouth of Big Barren Creek. Just after that, about noon, we came to Tucker Bay, where we had agreed to stop for lunch. Below Tucker Bay, Decker Chute takes off to the right in one of the wildest stretches on all of Current River. Here the water pitches into a rocky bank, with the whole entrance to the run blocked by a giant fallen sycamore and the rapid below it filled with treacherous sunken logs.

After we had beached the canoes and while the girls were laying out food for a cold luncheon, we explored the situation carefully. Over on the left a narrow and precarious-looking channel took off, but examination showed it to be completely blocked not far from its

entrance. In the righthand channel which carried most of the water, a short section had been sawed from the big sycamore log by some enterprising boatman to allow a comparatively safe passage. The trick with the canoes was to swing them around the worst snag on their stern lines then step aboard and "shoot the works."

The whole scene here was so wildy picturesque that we decided to try for movie shots of the canoes running the fast water. Nowhere on the trip, we knew, would we find a better location for these sequences. While we ate luncheon, we heard the roar of a powerful outboard, and upstream through the chute came a big John-boat with its pilot standing in the stern and navigating the swift currents with the skill and fine sense of touch of a cellist working over a difficult passage. Two passengers held down the front end of the boat so that it would draw a minimum of water.

The group turned out to be old man Wall, who lived down the river a mile or so, and his sons. They told us it was they who had sawed out the section of log and that, until they had done this, it had been necessary to "jump" a boat over the big sycamore in the middle where six inches of water went raging across it. The space where there was enough water to float a boat was approximately three feet wide, and the penalty for missing it could easily have been drowning.

After we'd finished luncheon, we paddled far up into Tucker Bay to see if we might glimpse a beaver from the colony that lived there. But the creatures are largely nocturnal and are seldom caught abroad in daylight, although there was ample sign of them in the willow and cottonwood cuttings. The low ground here, as at Gooseneck, was a mass of wildflowers; but here

the dominant species was a big mallow with blossoms of pink and white. Twenty members of this family are found in the Ozarks, some of them natives and some introduced species that escaped from the gardens of early settlers and became naturalized.

About two o'clock, when the sun had dropped enough to give fairly good lighting, we decided to try for our movie shots. Charles turned the stern paddle of their canoe over to Marian, braced his camera tripod in the bow, and went shooting down through the rapid to get background shots of the big log-jam and the water piling against it. Then he found an eddy where they could swing in to the shore below the right-angle bend and soon had his camera set up at a good vantage point. When his preparations were made, Ginnie and I ran the rapid in what turned out to be a fine fast-water movie sequence. Tiger, of course, was nonchalant about the whole affair, sitting as unconcernedly through the roughest part of the rapid as he does through the quietest pool.

The run from Tucker Bay to the mouth of Buffalo where we camped for the night is no more than five miles, and our most exciting moment of the afternoon was seeing a doe with a pair of well-grown twin fawns crossing the river in the shallows above the mouth of Little Barren Creek. This whole area along the Current was one of the first in the Missouri Ozarks to build its deer population back to normal.

We talked about this as we sat around the campfire that night, after supper was over and the dishes were washed and put away. Many of the things that happen in wild-land management are unexpected, and this has certainly been true of the growth of the Missouri

deer herd. In the beginning it was felt, on the basis of evidence from other states, that good forest management would increase the deer population by improving the habitat in the counties where there were still a few deer left. The largest area with such a remnant, granted this remnant was small, was along the wild and rugged Current River watershed.

In these timbered counties where we were creating our National Forest, fires were controlled and finally almost ended, and grazing by domestic animals on the public land was regulated. As this happened, the deer began to come back. A second big stimulus, as already pointed out, was the increase in preferred deer foods where the forest stands were opened up by removal of cull and weed trees. Although there are few areas in the Ozarks where the deer population has grown large enough to put real pressure on its food supply, we are probably arriving fairly close to the carrying capacity of these marginal lands.

The unexpected thing that has happened, of course, is the way in which the deer have taken over their old range in even the heavily settled agricultural counties in other parts of the state. Here they occupy the wood lots and small bands of timber along creeks and rivers. But because of the more fertile soils and the larger food supply in the wild and woodland border acres, as well as in cultivated fields, the deer population in these settled areas grows steadily. Today this population is still expanding, especially in the Ozark border counties and in the prairie lands north of the Missouri River.

This spread of the whitetails into the agricultural counties has created at least one odd problem. A thing which happens when we bring back a wild species such

as the deer—and no longer have natural predators to keep its numbers in balance with the range—is that the human hunter must take a calculated harvest each season. If this is not done, a population explosion will eventually occur, as has happened in many parts of the United States. When this happens, deer numbers suddenly outgrow the food supply. First young and then adult animals starve to death in ever-increasing numbers. The vitality of the entire herd is lowered, and finally the various species of food plants are so badly damaged that they may take a generation or more to recover.

We are glad this hasn't happened in Missouri; that biologists like Bob Dunkerson of the Conservation Commission and others have learned enough about whitetails and their management to prevent it. And yet right now we are concerned because an increasing percentage of our deer hunters are leaving the rugged and densely forested Ozark country to bag their annual deer out on the level lands. Here is less cover, less territory to be driven, fewer hills to climb. Often a party of hunters can put up at a comfortable motor court at the edge of a county-seat town and do their hunting entirely by automobile. So now we're trying to lure hunters back into the Ozark counties by pointing out that the sport of deer hunting can be artificialized until there's no sport left and that a trophy taken in the big timber has more value than one bagged at ten paces at a salt lick outside some farmer's barn lot. This is true, of course, but the real problem is that we want to harvest enough "wild land" deer to hold the Ozark herd to healthy size.

Long before we reached these conclusions beside our campfire at the mouth of Buffalo Creek, the girls had

sought their bedrolls and the mist was rolling up the river. We turned in and slept late, for on this last day we were in no hurry. Yet when I studied the topographic map after breakfast, I realized we still had a push of a dozen miles to reach our destination at Doniphan. Here our little outboard once more proved its worth. At mid-morning we lashed the three canoes together, with mine in the center. Then I pulled the starter cord, and away we went down river. Now and then when a rapid hove in sight, we would let go and each canoe would negotiate it individually. Then we would join up again and give it the gun through the quiet stretches.

In the last miles above the town are more signs of civilization. The Forest Service has established a camp and picnic ground on the riverbank which is much used, especially on weekends, by the people of the area. Lodges and clubhouses, a few of them quite elaborate, begin to dot the banks. The stream widens, and the pools of quiet water are longer. Yet this is still Current River, and at frequent intervals it picks up speed again. Even the last mile into the boat landing near the gravel pit below town is a swift and tricky rapid, swirling down between the piers of the highway bridge. We negotiated this successfully, however, and pulled in at our destination to find the boys waiting with the cars.

The sun beat down on the gravel bank where we unloaded and hauled the canoes out to drain. But once we had packed and were under way, we managed to cool off. Four hours later we were home again at Possum Trot with another leg of our journey completed—and this time we wouldn't have to rely on memory, for the record was filed away on color film. Now there was only

a single day's float to reach the Arkansas border where Current River leaves the Ozark foothills and runs out into the level lands that lead to the great flood plain of the Mississippi.

14 LAST STRETCH

If this leisurely summer journey of ours along Current River had taken us far from home, down some tributary of the McKenzie or the Peace rolling to the polar sea, our final day afloat would have been a sad one. It would have marked the end of an adventure that could be savored only once and thereafter lived in memory.

Fortunately for us, since we belong to Aldo Leopold's minority who "cannot live without wild things," the Current is a familiar river. It is hardly farther from our doorstep than were Thoreau's Merrimack and Concord from his; and even a hundred years later our stream has more of the wilderness flavor. We have floated the Current for thirty years without missing a single season. There have been one or two years when only in January and February have we failed to build campfires along the stream.

The Current has not changed markedly over this period, the great change having taken place in the time when the watershed was stripped of its virgin timber in one of the last midwestern orgies of "cut and get out." If anything, I would say that, although there are more highways touching it and a bridge or two across it that did not exist a quarter-century ago and more fishermen, things are looking up. Timber on at least part of the watershed is better managed. Forest fires have decreased greatly. Such farming as is done is probably being done a little more intelligently. There is more game, as I have pointed out in the case of the deer herd. There are a few

more fish in the river, perhaps as many as it will carry under present conditions of food, cover, water fluctuation, and fishing pressure. Good friends of mine will challenge this point, stating that the Current is vastly understocked. But we know that flood crests are not as high as they were thirty years ago, nor do the big rises come down as frequently as before the watershed began to heal. These are all good signs.

As I searched for records of old days along the Current, I recalled that Aldo Leopold, the great naturalist and ecologist, once had an interest in the Ozark country; indeed, he owned a cabin on the river near Doniphan which he and his brothers Carl and Fred used chiefly as a headquarters during the quail hunting season. In some excerpts from Aldo's early journals, which after his death his son Luna edited under the title *Round River,* there is the account of a ten-day float from Van Buren to Doniphan in November, 1926. It is purely a record of things killed, a typical hunter's daybook. But it could have been written this year, except for the increase in deer numbers already mentioned. The three Leopold brothers hunted quail, of which there were a fair number in the little fields bordering the river. They hunted turkeys, of which there were none, nor any sign. They saw not a single deer. But there were big swamp rabbits and plenty of squirrels for the pot and some bluegills, although no smallmouth bass are mentioned.

The really interesting thing about this account—which is, from beginning to end, the journal of a hunter interested almost solely in the game he is pursuing—is the way in which it contrasts with the later maturity of Aldo Leopold the man. In 1948, the same year in which he died tragically in a brush fire in Wisconsin, Leopold

finished compilation and editing of the thin volume of essays published under the title *A Sand County Almanac*. This small book is beyond any doubt the outstanding statement on the whole subject of conservation that has been made to date by any American. It is, moreover, a profound projection by a scientist into the fields of philosophy and ethics. It is perhaps the clearest exposition we have on the subject of ecology—of the relation of all living things to their environments. And finally, it is a literary gem, a felicitous statement by a disciplined humanist who had thought deeply on many subjects. It is a universe away from the journals of the young forester who, twenty years earlier, wrote within a narrow and circumscribed horizon.

There is a tendency among those who know the upper Current to assume that it becomes a dull and uninteresting stream in its lower reaches, beyond where the young Leopold floated. This is far from being true. Between Doniphan and the Arkansas line—and for a full day's float below this point—there is fine fishing water, and the river still runs swiftly and with tremendous power. It is naturally larger from the accretion of many springs and creeks that have joined it along its way. The valley grows steadily wider, and there is more farmland lying beyond the border of trees along the banks. Hills which rose steeply to heights of a thousand feet on the upper reaches are now gently rolling, with maximum elevations of no more than a hundred feet or so above the water. Nevertheless, despite losing the illusion of wilderness, we still find occasional high bluffs and enough gravel bars to provide good camping, granted they are spaced farther apart.

Since the distance to the Arkansas line can be nego-

tiated in a long day, we had decided to take advantage of an invitation from the Wright family of Doniphan to make our headquarters at their King Bee Lodge, an old but comfortable clubhouse which they had built on the riverbank many years ago. The lodge is located directly across from town and only a few hundred yards below the highway bridge, yet is as isolated as if it were in the wilderness.

The name "King Bee" intrigued us, and we inquired of the Wrights as to its origin. It turned out that this was the name of the first sawmill established in 1884 by Tom Wright, father of the big Wright family. King Bee was, in fact, not only a sawmill but also a small community that boasted a store, hotel, post office, and several homes. It was located on Little Black River, a tributary of the Current which parallels it some dozen miles to the east and joins it below the Arkansas border. Finally when the big timber within easy cutting distance of King Bee was gone—and the whole Ozark lumber business declined as the rafts of pine were floated down the Mississippi from Wisconsin and Minnesota—the Wrights moved to Doniphan and started a gravel screening operation which is their primary business today.

Big families are always interesting, and especially when they manage to stick together as the Wrights have done in Doniphan. Four Wrights are active in the business, another sister lives in the town, and two more bring their families back to visit frequently. What with husbands, wives, grandparents, children, and grandchildren, it isn't easy even to maintain your identity when you visit the Wrights of Doniphan. You find yourself adopted into the clan.

We made the three-hour drive south from Possum

Trot in late afternoon, and Joe and Bill Wright accompanied us across the river to King Bee, which we had never seen before. We were enchanted to find this isolated lodge buried in deep forest at the river's edge yet almost within calling distance of town. We unlocked the gate and drove along a gravel road where big trees closed in on both sides. At the lodge, which is set on high concrete pilings as safeguard against the floods that still roll down past Doniphan occasionally, we were greeted by a symphony of bird song. As I unpacked the car and Bill and I set the canoe on the ground beside it, I identified a half-dozen of the songsters.

The symphonic reception committee was led by the wood thrush, which Ginnie says always reminds her of swinging through the air in an old-fashioned rope swing. Among the instrumentalists were all of the mimics: catbird, brown thrasher, and mockingbird. A Carolina wren scolded from a corner of the lodge, and two indigo buntings flashed through the willows that lined the river. We had a cold toddy with Joe and Bill and a half-hour later joined the whole Wright family for a picnic at the Forest Service campground a few miles upstream from Doniphan. We drove there with T. L. Wright, who is one of Missouri's leading conservationists, and his brother-in-law Jerome Burford, another good companion on the river for many years.

One pleasant thing about picnics is that they generally end at a reasonable hour. Long before ten o'clock we were bedded down at King Bee, lulled to sleep by the singing of the river, the distant hooting of a barred owl, and the oft-repeated call of the whip-poor-will.

When I woke next morning, the mist was heavy above the river, drifting gently upstream on some vagrant

current of air. The first rays of the rising sun came horizontally through the trees, and a green heron flew past, attracting attention to himself by his unmistakable "guok, guok." We were in no great hurry this morning; yet the day was too fine to waste abed, and soon I had the coffee boiling and bacon sizzling in the skillet. Running water and the electric stove in the kitchen at King Bee were a far cry from our cooking fires on the gravel bars throughout the past four months.

When breakfast was over, it was still not much after six o'clock. Ginnie cleared away the dishes while I hauled the canoe to the water's edge and slid it down the twenty-foot bank to the river. The current rolled past, swift and deep, but I managed to tie up to the willows in a small eddy where we could load without too much difficulty. After all the years, I still found myself surprised by the amount of gear that goes along on even such a short trip as this. I looked at the room which all this gear occupied and wondered how we ever managed to add to it the equipment necessary to live for a week on the river; yet I knew from long experience it could be done. We locked up the lodge, took a final look around to be sure nothing essential was forgotten, and stepped aboard our craft. One strong push with the stern paddle sent us out into the swift current, and we were off on the final leg of our summer's journey down Current River.

It is on this last stretch of the river that the illusion of wilderness begins to fade. On either side we start to see lodges, clubhouses, and resorts. Many of these are in good taste, built of logs or stone that fit well into the environment. Some are quite elaborate, with flower beds and carefully mowed lawns, which seem somehow out of place. Yet these things cannot change the essence of

the early morning river when the pileated woodpecker comes winging strongly across above our heads. Even the big John-boat driven by its powerful outboard and picking its way up through a rapid somehow fits into the scene. This is no fancy speedboat but a working craft that has developed through the years to serve a specific purpose.

We pass one high bluff where the scars of the old log-slide that almost certainly has not been used for fifty years are plainly visible. This was where the logs were hauled to a high point and then skidded down to be rafted to the sawmill. But the history of this part of Current River goes back farther than the days of early logging, for it was along in this region somewhere that De Soto and his ragged army must have crossed as they headed northward into the granite country of the St. Francois Mountains. Spanish coins and a few pieces of old armor have been found to the south of Doniphan; and there is even a tale that the big razorback hogs once found in these foothills and the swamplands to the east were the descendents of the herd that De Soto's men hazed along before them as a final hedge against scurvy and starvation.

There are minor changes in the flora as Current River hurries along toward its destination in the level lands of the White River flood plain. The Spanish moss and mistletoe have already been mentioned, both of these being more typical of the southland than of our Ozark hills. And now, about midway between Doniphan and the Arkansas line, we note the first cypress trees. This is a species belonging to the low-lying swamps along the St. Francis and the Mississippi bottoms, but it begins to appear here on the Current at a point called Big Island.

There are few large springs along this lower river, and most of the small ones we saw on our day's float issued from the rocky bluffs and were equipped with an iron pipe for convenience. But since we didn't know the location of the safe ones, we stuck to our water jug. There was no decrease in the number of small songbirds, but we saw almost none of the larger species that add interest to the upper river. Whether this is from the gradual thinning out of the forest and greater amount of cultivated land would be difficult to say. Of the small green herons there were plenty, and an occasional kingfisher. But there was no sign of the osprey, and the day brought only a single pair of red-tailed hawks. There were no great blue herons or little blues or American egrets. Nor did we see the anhinga, or water turkey, which nests in the Reelfoot Lake country and is generally fairly common on the lower Current in late summer.

We stopped for luncheon where a little cut-off ran around a small island and joined the river again after perhaps a half-mile. Here at the upper end was shade, and the blue water in the cut-off looked as though it might produce some sunfish and even a small bass or two. Sure enough, when I tied a tiny white metal and feather lure onto Ginnie's leader that had been sent to us by a friend in Birmingham with the assurance panfish could not resist it, we found we could hardly make a cast without a strike. Some of the fish hooked were returned to the water, but several were large enough to keep. And there's no telling how many we might have taken—except that, after hanging the lure up in the treetops and snagging it down among the sunken logs and rescuing it each time with infinite pains, I finally lured a largemouth of good size into striking. But by this time the light

leader had evidently become frayed, and the bass made a rush and snapped it, carrying our lucky lure down to his home beneath the logs.

The truth is that fishing was not a prime objective of our day. Yet the bass were striking, and when such days come along, it is impossible not to respond. By mid-afternoon we had a good mess of smallmouths of fair size all cleaned and scaled and stored away in the icebox, along with the sunnies we had taken earlier. At three o'clock, in the heat of the afternoon, we stopped in a swift-water run for a cool swim. And then, because I hadn't been down this stretch of river for many years and was somewhat vague about the distance we still had to travel, I started up the motor and we sped downstream at a good clip. The water is still swift, but there are few obstructions, so that we made good time and came at four-thirty to the Arkansas line (an entirely imaginary one), where Jerome Burford was waiting for us with the car.

Soon we were packed and on our way back to Doni-phan: first over a mile of gravel road and then, as we crossed into Missouri, picking up a good blacktop high-way. Our day's float down the river had taken eight hours; our trip by car back to Doniphan and King Bee took no more than thirty minutes; but this is a phenome-non that happens often when you travel the Ozark streams. It had been a fine day, at any rate, and a good way to end our Current River season.

15 KILOWATTS, PROGRESS, AND OTHER THREATS

What future lies ahead for Current River and for other American streams that have managed to retain their original beauty and, more especially, some of the quality of wilderness? Shall we try to save them so that the generation of our grandchildren may know something of what our country was like in the beginning? Or is it at all important that they should understand and recognize the raw materials out of which we have built our civilization?

How we answer these questions depends on what we believe. Is the thing we call progress subject to the law of diminishing returns, or is the destruction of everything in America that is natural and free and wild a matter of no moment? For those indifferent to destruction, the houses dotting a new subdivision will always be preferable to trees standing in a forest; while another kilowatt of electricity to help mine the resources of an area will be considered as the ultimate good.

Those who are not indifferent find other values worth weighing. There is the value of wild land for science, to be used as a yardstick in measuring the health of tame land. There is its value for the preservation of wildlife and for the recreation of our people. And finally comes the matter of esthetics—that renewal of the spirit which we know comes from association with unspoiled nature. Fortunately there is always a minority who believe these scientific, recreational, wildlife, and spiritual values are

important—and who will work and fight to preserve them.

As has been pointed out more than once in these pages, the feeling of wilderness which we get as our canoe drifts silently down the quiet reaches of the Current or shoots swiftly through its rapids is at least partly an illusion. This is not true wilderness, for people have lived here since the early years of the last century. Moreover, land-use along this watershed during the past fifty years has been about as bad as it could be. Cut-and-get-out logging, wildfire in the woods, overgrazing and poor farming methods on land that should never be farmed—all these have combined to cause a huge volume of gravel erosion and to accentuate the effects of flood and drought.

Despite these evils, the Current has suffered no pollution from a concentration of population along its banks. Here is a stream that flows as pure and undefiled as it did on the first day the white man saw it, and this alone, considering its accessibility, would make it worth preserving for all time. Because so much of the shoreline of the stream is steep and forested, with little land suitable for cultivation, it has been able to maintain much of its wild character. It seems probable, moreover, that the ecological low point was reached in the Current River country some twenty years ago and that conditions have since been slowly improving. The most important single factor here has been the virtual elimination of large-scale forest fires, which has allowed the humus layer to start building again on the floor of the woodland that covers 90 per cent of the watershed.

This layer of organic matter, after a short period of years, begins to hold the rain and slow the run-off,

thereby checking erosion. But, in addition, considerable land along the watershed has come under good forest management, especially that included in the Missouri National Forests and smaller amounts in the hands of the state and a few individual landowners who practice good forestry. There is, if anything, a smaller acreage being farmed along the river valley. Only the load of free-roaming livestock in the forest is still heavy and destructive.

On balance it would appear today that biological conditions along Current River are improving. The humus layer reduces soil impaction and this not only checks erosion but increases the in-soak and insures greater ground storage of water. Springs that feed the river become more stable, and this, in turn, means a more even flow in the stream itself. The highs and lows of flood and drought are moderating. All these things, finally, result in better life conditions within the stream, starting with the aquatic plants and continuing through the entire biotic pyramid that includes insects, crustaceans, and fish up to the smallmouth bass that is the climax species in the river. The same thing holds for plant life along the banks and for the many forms of wildlife.

Chances are, under normal conditions, this improvement would continue and might even keep pace with an increased use of the Current River area for recreation. There are, however, alternatives to this slow but fairly steady improvement of the Current River watershed in its present use for forestry, small-scale farming, wildlife habitat, and recreation; and these should be examined.

Of the many threats to the few free-running, unspoiled streams of America, the greatest comes from the Corps of Engineers of the United States Army. The reason for

this is simply that, through an extension of their powers and responsibility for the management and improvement of rivers and harbors, the Engineers have become the world's greatest dam builders. They construct dams for flood control, for navigation, for power generation, and even for recreation. They have plans completed or under way for damming practically every running stream in the United States at a total cost that staggers the imagination even in an atomic age.

Since the worst thing which can happen to a free-running river is to stop it from running, it follows that the greatest threat comes from the Army Engineers who would dam everything. Yet there are certain fallacies in the entire water-management philosophy of their vast bureaucratic organization. Although there are mechanical results from damming a river, there are also biological or ecological results. The Engineers have to date shown themselves long on engineering and mechanics but short on knowledge of biology and ecology.

There is another fallacy in much of the Army Engineers' planning, and this has to do with their belief in the "multiple purpose" dam that is built for flood control, power, and recreation. This fallacy is easily demonstrated by pointing out that a power dam must be operated at "high pool" to produce electricity. A flood-control dam, on the other hand, must be operated at "low pool" to allow room for the flood waters that come rolling down. And finally, the structure built for conservation and recreation should have a "stable pool" to enable fish to spawn, prevent the creation of great mud flats, and allow for the construction of recreational facilities where they will not be alternately flooded out or left high and dry, a mile away from water across those

mud flats. This is, perhaps, a slight oversimplification; yet its logic will be immediately apparent.

The backing which the Army Engineers receive in Washington is not difficult to trace. It can be guessed at by surveying the interests which benefit from dam building. Here are the big contractors in several fields of construction, manufacturers of heavy dirt-moving equipment, the cement industry, electrical-equipment manufacturers—to name only a few. These influences added together are enough to give the Engineers an unbeatable lobby and to push huge pork-barrel bills practically unopposed through every session of Congress. These make even the most extravagant dam-building schemes exceedingly difficult to defeat.

The first proposal to dam Current River came in the mid-1930's when the Army submitted its original flood-control proposal for the White River in Arkansas, with similar proposals covering the watersheds of most Missouri streams. The effort got as far as an enabling act passed by Congress which authorized the eventual construction of some thirty "high dams" on the rivers of Missouri. This is all that the Army ever asks initially, since it may not get around to wanting the money for a specific dam for a generation but can always go after an individual appropriation where the specific dam has been authorized.

In the case of some Missouri dams, studies indicated they were needed, and several have been built. In the Ozark highland of Missouri and north Arkansas there are dams on the St. Francis, the Black, the North Fork, and White River. The dams on the latter two streams are the largest and include Norfork, Bull Shoals, and Table Rock, which create lakes of tremendous size. Lake Wap-

papelo, created by the St. Francis dam, is silting at a high rate and has not done a successful flood-control job. Clearwater on Black River is somewhat more successful, although the entire story here will not be known for some years. One thing that happens on these smaller reservoirs with excessive siltation is that, as they fill up with earth and gravel, their storage capacity shrinks. This makes necessary a faster draw-down in time of flood, so that eventually the valley below the dam is flooding as badly —or perhaps worse—than before the dam was built.

There were two dams proposed for Current River in the original plan and authorized in the enabling act. From the very beginning, however, strong opposition developed to these dams, not only along the valley but throughout the entire state of Missouri. A Current River Protective Association was formed shortly after 1940 and has remained in existence to this day in skeleton form, beating down every attempt by the Engineers and small groups of promotors and land speculators to put the dams through for final appropriations from Congress.

At meetings held throughout the area, the Engineers failed signally in one attempt after another to justify the Current River dams. It was shown by their opponents that the proposed structures would affect flood levels on White River imperceptibly and on the Mississippi not at all; that the stream flow was insufficient to furnish an economical source of steady electrical power; that existing gravel erosion would result in disastrous siltation not only in the reservoirs but far upstream; and that the "cost to benefit" ratio even on the basis of early low-cost estimates was ridiculously high.

This fight to prevent Current River from being dammed went on for several years, and it was not until

1954 that definite steps were taken by an authorized body to drop the dams. At this time the Arkansas-White-Red River Basins Inter-Agency Committee adopted a resolution presented by the Governor of Missouri. This was to the effect that, because of unanimous recommendations by all the state agencies and the Water Use and Control Group of the Inter-Agency Committee, the Current River dams should not be built. The Committee then recommended, as an integral part of the Arkansas-White-Red Basins plan, the following:

1. That in lieu of reservoir development, Current River be kept as a free-flowing stream and developed as a recreational area through co-operative state and federal action.

2. That a co-operative survey be made by state and federal agencies to prepare a master plan designed to preserve and enhance the natural qualities of the stream.

One thing which the Inter-Agency Committee did not do—and indeed may not have been empowered to do—was to press for actual de-authorization of the Current River dams by Congress. Until this is done, the Engineers can actually proceed to build them if hearings can be held so quietly that they fail to arouse the opposition and if they can get Congress to appropriate the money. Typical of what can happen under present conditions is a new drive started during the summer of 1958 by a small group of promotors to again petition the Engineers to build the dams. As this is written, it seems safe to say that little will come of the present effort. Yet the group is circulating petitions throughout the counties on the watershed and claiming vast benefits from imaginary low-cost power and an influx of giant industries, not to mention

the period of good times during the two or three construction years.

One thing of considerable value did follow the recommendations of the Inter-Agency Committee, although to date no action has been taken on it. A study was made in which the National Park Service co-operated with the Missouri Conservation Commission, the State Park Board, and the Division of Resources and Development. This study resulted in a preliminary report called *Plan for Preservation and Development of Recreational Resources—Current and Eleven Point River Country of Missouri.* This report, which was published and distributed by the Missouri Division of Resources and Development, contains much valuable information as to recreational possibilities in the eastern Ozarks. Neither the plan nor its recommendations are entirely definitive. They were not meant to be. Rather, they furnish the basis for further study and discussion by everyone interested in the area. It seems too early to say whether the recommendations are either fully backed by sound research or would prove practical in the long run. On the whole, however, the report is a start and a fairly good one on a recreational plan for the Current River country.

Perhaps the thing most lacking in all considerations of the use which can be made of the Ozark area as a whole is the ecological approach. The Conservation Commission thinks largely in terms of wildlife, the State Forestry Division in terms of fighting fire, the U. S. Foresters in terms of "multiple use"—and the public as a whole does not think about the matter at all. We know today beyond any doubt, however, that the use which is to be made of land—be it a small watershed, a state, a nation, or our planet—must finally depend on its capabilities for sup-

porting life. This would seem to be one of Nature's immutable laws, if such things exist; and certainly we can see it in action wherever we look in the world today.

As we turn back to study our own years of experience in the Ozark country, it seems possible to make certain observations. First of all, in the wilderness state the area supported a rich complex of plant and animal life, this probably resulting from its extreme age, geographical location, and comparatively favorable climate. Yet because the Ozark soils are, on the whole, basically poor and with a low life-carrying capacity, there have always been limits on the numbers of each individual species which the area supported. When the white man came, many of these species could not stand the pressure exerted upon them and were rapidly reduced to the point of extinction. Yet in spite of this, limited numbers of a surprising variety of them still exist in the area.

The carrying capacity of the Ozarks is as limited for man as for other species. The primary plant resource is the forest, which does not and never will produce great quantities of food for the higher animals, among them domestic animals and man. This condition is not going to change in any large degree. The forest resource can be vastly improved and in this case will yield a richer harvest and support more people. Income from agriculture will continue low and may even decline from its present sorry estate, since it is more difficult here than almost anywhere to increase the size of farm holdings or to operate these more efficiently. There are some areas that seem to promise a certain amount of mining development; and though this will mean an increase in employment, most of the wealth produced by the mines will move swiftly out of the Ozarks.

Thus it seems clear that the future of the Current River lies in its development for forestry, for the production of wildlife (including fish, birds, and mammals), and for such recreation as hunting, fishing, camping, and canoeing. Even in recreation, it seems to me, there have always been and will always be limitations. Ozark summers are hot, with temperatures regularly moving into the high nineties and with protracted dry spells in late summer and autumn. The ideal times of year are from early April through June and from early September until frost. Since this does not correspond closely with the normal vacation season, there are some limits to the number of people who will vacation here. Weekends are always a possibility, however, and the Current River country is within weekend driving distance for a large number of people.

The present facilities for vacationists and weekend recreationists are severely limited in scope and quality; and a reason for this is undoubtedly that the demand for better accommodations has never really existed. As always in such cases, there are exceptions to this statement. State parks, motor courts, and cottages can be found if one searches them out. There are also a limited number of good campgrounds, some of which have been mentioned in earlier chapters.

Another thing which will always limit the number of people who use an area such as Current River for recreation is that it can be enjoyed best by floating down it in a boat or canoe, camping as you go. This is a sport that not everyone enjoys or is fitted by experience or temperament to participate in. The river, moreover, is cold and swift and does not make an ideal playground for young children unless their parents are experienced outdoor people. Finally, as long as the Ozarks contain a large

population of free-roaming livestock, such pests as chiggers and ticks will penalize any foray into the summer woods.

Once these limitations of the Current River country as a recreational area have been set down, it should be pointed out that—with the exception of the insect pests —many of them are the very qualities for which the river should be preserved and which should be the objectives of any plan for its development. Just as the Maine coast, the pine woods of the north country, the western mountains, and the big impoundments of the Tennessee Valley each has its appeal for certain groups of recreation seekers—so do the vast springs, the steep forested hollows, great limestone bluffs, deep pools, and swift rapids of Current River. And just as steps have been taken to develop these other areas for recreation, so should we work to save this most beautiful of the Ozark rivers.

The need to preserve areas that are wild and natural increases in America with each day that goes by; for it has been truly said that "wilderness is a resource which can shrink but never grow." We have made a start through the State and National Park systems, the National Monuments, and the creation of "primitive and wilderness areas" in the National Forests. Yet the pressure increases daily on these resources, and we have made only a start. Every region has its "Current Rivers." The time grows short in which to save them and develop them for the use of all Americans who love the outdoors.

The Nature Conservancy, which has a nation-wide interest in these matters, recently made the sound proposal that the country should have National Rivers, just as it has National Parks, and that these should be set aside as inviolate. Such a proposal would be ideal for Current

River, which we will continue to work to preserve as a wild and natural free-flowing stream. The danger to this little wilderness at our doorstep lies in the juggernaut called progress, which takes no account of natural values. We have fought and will continue to fight for such values because they are necessary and because our grandsons have a right to know them.

With luck, the time when I can no longer wield a canoe paddle lies some years ahead. Thus for many more seasons Ginnie and I hope to see the tiers of dogwood blossoms covering the Ozark hills like a May snow and to see the oaks flaming into color in October. We hope to run our canoe down the wild water and drink from the crystal springs, to startle the osprey from his high aerie and the deer from among the lily pads. On summer nights, we want to camp on the high, clean gravel bars and watch the reflected stars that seem to move upstream.

EPILOGUE

Much has happened in the Current River country since we saw the last page of *Stars Upstream* set into type. Most important is that our dream of making a "national river" out of our favorite Ozark stream has become a reality. The Current is, today, America's *first* "national river."

The path leading to this reality has been neither smooth nor easy. Yet in the end a group of dedicated Missouri conservationists, aided by members of the Missouri delegation in the Congress and by the National Park Service under Director George Hartzog, secured passage of Public Law 88-492 creating the Ozark National Scenic Riverways under Park Service direction.

The law reads as follows: "... for the purpose of conserving and interpreting unique scenic and other natural values, including preservation of portions of Current River and Jacks Fork River as free-flowing streams, preservation of springs and caves, management of wildlife, and provision for the use and enjoyment of the outdoor recreation resources thereof by the people of the United States ...".

Today the task of *establishing* the riverways is almost finished. If my own hopes for it are realized, it will be because the National Park Service in its planning gives full consideration to the ecological capabilities of this magnificent area. As pointed out in my final paragraphs, preservation of the Current and Jacks Fork rivers depends on full realization of the

life-supporting limitations of these fragile watersheds. Here, overdevelopment for human use will surely mean destruction rather than the preservation that is specified by the law. The responsibility here is not a light one.

LEONARD HALL
Chairman, Advisory Commission
Ozark National Scenic Riverways, and
Trustee, National Parks Association

Possum Trot Farm
January, 1969

D1600790